PRAISE FOR
The Black Family's Guide to College Admissions

"There are many books that provide insight on the college admissions process, but none is specifically geared toward Black families. There are things that Black families should know as they go through the college search and selection process, and this book provides direction and clear answers."

—JAWAAN J. WALLACE, Dean of College Counseling, Marlborough School

"A unique, refreshing, and much-needed resource from two admissions insiders. This book is a tremendously valuable guide for Black students and their families as they seek to make informed decisions, ask astute questions, and ultimately select the best college for them."

—RICK CLARK, Assistant Vice Provost / Executive Director of Undergraduate Admission, Georgia Institute of Technology; coauthor of *The Truth about College Admission*

"I appreciate that Fields and Herndon-Brown consider the intersection of race and the value of the HBCU. This book is a must-read for Black students and their families. I now feel more prepared for my own three children to begin the process."

—ERIN ROSE, parent and Florida A&M University graduate

"I am confident *The Black Family's Guide to College Admissions* will become a valuable resource for counselors, mentors, and others who are a sounding board of reason in the lives of graduating seniors and their families, especially for first-generation college-goers, who will need to create realistic options for themselves."

—L. M. ROZIERS, President, Mitch22 Foundation, Inc.

"Essential reading for anyone who works with Black students considering college. The authors share invaluable insight into the complex and necessary concerns that Black families must consider when exploring higher education, lived experiences shared by too few in college admissions."

—**MARIE BIGHAM**, Founder, ACCEPT: Admissions Community Cultivating Equity & Peace Today

"This is a great addition to the pantheon of reading material in the arena of college admissions. I'm not aware of a book that specifically targets Black families; this was a welcome and necessary read."

—**CLEO A.**, parent of rising junior

"To find a book on the college admissions process that is genuine, professional, and realistic is amazing. When that same book is helpful for students, parents, school counselors, counselor educators, and grad students, it's a rarity. To have that book amplify the Black student experience is powerful and needed."

—**KATHERINE MATHEWS**, National Certified School Counselor

"A must-have guide that should be read by every Black parent, educator, and school counselor tasked with advising Black students, long before they embark on the college admissions process."

—**CATHLEEN TRIGG-JONES**, Emmy Award–winning journalist, mother of four, Founder of iWoman TV

THE
Black Family's
Guide to
College
Admissions

A CONVERSATION ABOUT
EDUCATION, PARENTING, AND RACE

TIMOTHY L. FIELDS AND
SHEREEM HERNDON-BROWN

JOHNS HOPKINS UNIVERSITY PRESS
Baltimore

© 2022 Johns Hopkins University Press
All rights reserved. Published 2022
Printed in the United States of America on acid-free paper
9 8 7 6 5 4 3 2

Johns Hopkins University Press
2715 North Charles Street
Baltimore, Maryland 21218-4363
www.press.jhu.edu

Cataloging-in-Publication Data is available from the Library of Congress

ISBN 978-1-4214-4489-5 (paperback)
ISBN 978-1-4214-4490-1 (ebook)

A catalog record for this book is available from the British Library.

Special discounts are available for bulk purchases of this book. For more information, please contact Special Sales at specialsales@jh.edu.

I dedicate this book to Regent Elridge McMillan and his lifelong dedication to promoting educational access and equality and to the lives of Ramone Harper, Noah Johnson, and Myron Burney, who were living testaments that success has more than one path! #TB4L

TLF

To all my former students at Brooklyn Friends School, Westtown School, Riverdale Country School, and Trinity School—I wrote this for you. When you got into your top-choice colleges, I celebrated, and when you didn't, I blamed myself. I could have and should have done more. You drive me to serve my online community and private clients with brutal honesty and relentless effort.

To my children—Sydney, Kerry, Sai, and Samara. My only wish is that you make a contribution to this world as I am trying to do, in your way, and with your style. Just promise me that you'll celebrate being young, gifted, and Black.

To my wife, Keri—Howard. 1911. 1999. 4ever$.

SHB

Contents

Preface

On a beautiful January day in 2021 in Washington, DC, a small crowd gathered for the inauguration of Joseph R. Biden as the forty-sixth president of the United States. Although this day, in many ways, was overshadowed by the outgoing president, a tragic domestic terrorist attack on the Capitol earlier that month, and the continuance of the global pandemic that limited attendance and had taken the lives of millions worldwide, there was still so much to celebrate on this historic occasion. With the world watching, we as a country were all able to witness a peaceful transfer of power with several notable Black figures in the crowd, including the first female vice president of the United States, Kamala Harris, who identifies as Black and Indian. Vice President Harris is also the first vice president to have graduated from a Historically Black College and University (HBCU), Howard University, the same school that US Supreme Court Justice Thurgood Marshall had attended for law school years before and which is less than three miles away from the Capitol steps where she was sworn in.

On the dais on this momentous occasion were members of Congress, celebrities, and family members of the elected officials. Among the crowd was the first Black president, Barack Obama, who started his undergraduate education at Occidental College and then transferred to Columbia University. (Occidental is a private predominantly white institution [PWI] in Los Angeles, CA, with 1,839 undergraduates and no graduate students.) He was joined by his wife, former First Lady Michelle Obama, who attended Princeton University. Also attending was Congressman Jim Clyburn, a major catalyst in the election of the new president, donning his South Carolina State University baseball cap and showing great pride in his home state and his HBCU alma mater. Many would argue, though, that the climax of the day was the powerful poem delivered by Amanda Gorman, national youth poet laureate, who attended Harvard College. We mention where these individuals went to college because, for many of us, college is a badge of honor. While there were many others there that day, we highlight these individuals because of the variety in the educational choices they made that may have influenced why they were on that stage on that significant day.

Just as they arrived at their success by different college pathways, many individuals achieve success without going to a well-known or selective college or without going to college at all. The goal of most parents is for their children to live healthy lives, be good citizens, and ultimately become successful, however they may choose to define it. Some define success by simply being admitted to college; others by graduating with a college degree and acquiring accolades and titles through their accomplishments; but most measure success by the amount of money they make. No matter how success is defined, college is usually a part of that equation, as evidenced by President Obama, former First Lady Michelle Obama, Vice President Harris, Congressman Clyburn, and Amanda Gorman. While all of them had different opportunities and life circumstances that may have influenced where they went to college, they all decided to go. Despite differences in resources, size, location, and institutional type, each of the schools offered something that allowed them to grow and experience success in their careers. Did they know when they chose their school, with the help maybe of a parent, college counselor, or family friend, that they would end up on that stage that day as a part of history? Probably not, but the fact that they attended such different universities says a lot about the unique higher education system we have in this country, which offers so many opportunities to students looking for a college education. Such variety is not the case in many parts of the world.

However great the school they attended, that choice did not determine their presence on that stage; rather, the key was what they did with the opportunities afforded to them both in college and beyond. As parents, it is essential that you and your child understand the choices that are in front of them. Whether they choose to go to college, aspire to be an artist or athlete, or have entrepreneurial courage and drive, you know your child best, and as they enter their formative years, you can probably tell the path they are on, given their abilities, talents, and other characteristics. *College is not for everyone*, and the path to and through college can be difficult. The multiple decisions that go into it, especially for Black families, have multiple layers that extend beyond simply choosing which college to apply to and attend.

How Did We Come to Write This Book?

In June of 2020, a few weeks after the tragic slaying of George Floyd, the entire country was trying to deal with both the tragedy that had occurred in Minneapolis and the reality that violent racism was still alive and thriving in America long after the end of segregation. While many wanted to view what happened to George Floyd as an isolated incident, his death was one in a long series of unarmed Black people who died at the hands of police. These deaths provided a reality check and awakening for a country that had turned a blind eye to injustices for far too long. Throughout the country, people of all backgrounds took to the streets to protest, signaling that these acts of injustice and racism could no longer be tolerated.

At the same time that millions were taking to the streets in protest, an online movement began in Atlanta and quickly spread nationally. Brave young Black people took to social media to express their anger and frustration at their affluent private schools for their blatant racism or for being complicit in microaggressions by white students and faculty. Thanks to the accelerated pace of social media, there soon were black@INSERTPRIVATESCHOOL posts from schools across the country that documented instances of racism against Black students. And it hurt us to read them.

We are both Black parents, and although we have made different choices about our children's schools, all of the six children between us have gone to predominantly white schools. We attended predominantly white high schools ourselves: public (Tim) and private

(Shereem). The feelings expressed in those Instagram posts, the fear, anger, and isolation, hit very close to home. As we read the posts of students, we knew they were giving voice to truths we had known for most of our adult lives. We also knew that we had to use our voices to amplify theirs and address one of the most common themes in the posts: college counseling.

We have known each other for almost a decade from working in the college admissions profession. One of us (Shereem) was an admissions officer at Georgetown University and has been a college counselor at two prestigious private schools. Given his experiences on both sides, secondary school and collegiate, he started his own independent consulting company to help families think about everything from course selection to testing options to which institutions to visit to writing application essays. In sum, his company guides families step-by-step through the entire application process up to the point when they decide what school the student will attend. The other (Tim) works on the college side as the senior associate dean of admissions at Emory University, where he spends the majority of time recruiting, reviewing applications, and building programming to promote access, not just at Emory, but for all students looking to attend a postsecondary education institution. Tim's experience is extensive as he has collaborated as an admissions expert with national educational organizations such as QuestBridge, the Jack Kent Cooke Foundation, the United Negro College Fund, and the National Merit Scholarship Corporation, in addition to having worked closely with several Federal TRiO Programs for many years.

We became friends and supported each other's writing and professional efforts. We learned that we had contrasting educational backgrounds. Shereem attended boarding school and Wesleyan University (a PWI), and Tim attended public school and Morehouse College (an HBCU). Shereem is a first-generation college graduate whose parents were both blue-collar workers, and Tim is a fourth-generation college graduate whose parents have higher education administration experience. We found it interesting that our radically different educational experiences had brought us to a similar place.

Given the racial reckoning that was happening around us, we had the momentum and motive to write something that would address the inequities we see in our personal and professional experiences in college admissions. These inequities were the subjects of so many black@INSERTPRIVATESCHOOL posts. Black students at private schools were consistently mentioning the many racial disparities in college counseling that white and Black students received. While every school may be different, the college counseling process and the guidance given to students should be the same:

- Choose appropriate classes and do well in them.
- Take standardized tests (SAT and ACT).
- Get involved in the community through activities in the arts, athletics, or volunteerism.
- Get a balanced college list from your school counselor that matches your strengths and interests.
- Have counselor and parents meet to make sure everyone is on the same page.
- Write and revise self-reflective essays.
- Get feedback on the essays from counselor, teachers, and parents.
- Feel supported.
- And, in the end, have college options.

That seems simple, right? Well, the black@INSERTPRIVATESCHOOL posts told a different story. Here are a few posts about college counseling at some of the most prestigious private schools in the country:

"My college counselor told me I would never get into an Ivy league school. She looked at my transcript and told me I did not have enough Honors and AP courses. I had 4 but that was not enough. No one ever told me how much I needed, or I would have taken more."

"My dad is a single father and worked a lot. He could not come to my college meetings. When I talked to my college counselor, she

told me I should just apply to state schools because of financial aid. She never told me that many private colleges are need blind and may have wanted me for diversity based on my race and class. I felt that she dismissed me because my dad was not in her face."

"When I asked my college counselor about Spelman, he told me that I should not go to a Black school because the world is not Black. I told him that all the schools he was suggesting were white and that the world wasn't white either. He barely spoke to me after that, and I only got into a few colleges and ended up transferring later on."

As the posts surfaced, it became overwhelming for us as Black parents and college admissions professionals to read them. We knew that what was being shared was true because, unfortunately, we had seen and experienced it.

When I (Shereem) was a school counselor at two private schools, the undermatching of students of color—Black and Latinx—happened all the time. And what is *undermatching*? Undermatching is when a school counselor poorly evaluates a student's chances for admission. It's when they suggest colleges that are not good matches for a student because they failed to consider the student's strengths, interests, aspirations, culture, or family dynamics. An undermatched college list includes only schools the counselor is familiar with or was generated by an algorithm such as CollegeXpress or BigFuture. Black students undermatching infuriates me. It's one thing if they choose to apply to those schools, but when they are not presented with all of their options, that is unacceptable given all the colleges and universities out there. Black families who are spending money, and perhaps sacrificing cultural acceptance, for their child to attend a private school deserve better.

With what was happening in the United States in summer 2020, we knew that a book specifically for Black parents was needed. Yes, there are already tons of books out there about college admissions that will help with essay writing, provide procedural guidance through the standard application process, increase standardized test scores, and supply rankings and overviews of colleges. What we felt was missing from the college admissions literature, however, is a book that speaks directly to Black families and addresses issues that matter to us and have been overlooked—issues such as grappling with the idea of placing your student in a primary or secondary school where very few people will look like them, or the long-standing debate in many Black homes about the cultural and educational credibility of HBCUs compared with PWIs. Several books and organizations are specifically designed for first-generation Black college students, but we have not come across any books or programs designed for the "Black-ish" population, a reference to the ABC network show starring Tracee Ellis Ross and Anthony Anderson. By Black-ish, we mean those who went to college and are now making difficult decisions about where we live and send our children to school. We are the Black generation that has, at times, made choices that set our children up for micro- and macro-aggressions at affluent public and private schools that claim to be "allies" and "diverse."

Black-ish is a funny yet bold television show, created by Kenya Barris (Clark Atlanta University), about a Black father's determination to establish a sense of cultural identity in his family while living in a predominantly white and affluent environment. Starring Anthony Anderson (Howard University) and Tracee Ellis Ross (Brown University).

We wrote this book for the Black families who feel uninformed, overlooked, and in some instances ignored in the college admissions process. We also wrote this book for educators who work with Black students and families. We are hopeful that those who call themselves guidance counselors, school counselors, or college advisors are looking for more insight and resources with the goal of truly believing and investing in diversity, equity, and inclusivity. The search for the right college is personal, but for Black families, given the history of this country and the foundation of the educational system, some additional issues must be considered. We want to bring these issues to the forefront and provide some context around them. While conversations about the issues have been going on for years in small circles, they need to happen more widely and with many more participants. We wrote this book for Black parents like us who strive to do what's best for our children with more resources perhaps than we were raised with. Many of us struggle to know what the "best" education looks like for our Black children when we want them to be secure in their culture and identity but also to get a quality education. Our aim is to explain how college admissions works and what Black parents need to think about as they puzzle through how to educate their children at the best schools possible. These are not easy conversations for families to have because many Black college graduates maintain that their children *must* attend the same kind of institution they did, if not better. Some of us who went to PWIs—especially in the Northeast or on the West Coast— are curious about HBCUs, but since attending an HBCU wasn't our experience, we can easily turn to the college rankings of *U.S. News and World Report* to arbitrate what is best. In our two households we have graduates from both PWIs and HBCUs: Shereem's wife attended Howard University, and Tim's wife went to the University of Miami.

Yes, we are college admissions experts who have spent thousands of hours working with families to help them navigate the college admissions process, but we are parents first. We know firsthand that this discussion about what is the best college for our children is complicated and needs to start earlier. We do not claim to have all the answers, but we do know that we have a lot of information. Black students and families deserve better, and we hope to offer what we know to help anyone who will listen. We no longer want to talk only among ourselves. Instead, we want to grow a community by encouraging these conversations about Black families and our educational choices for our children. We invite you to join us.

The Black Family's Guide
to College Admissions

Introduction

If you are reading this book looking for the magic formula to get your child into their dream school, this is not the book for you. There is a saying in the profession of college admissions: "it's an art, not a science," meaning that it's a much more nuanced decision than one driven by numbers. Many would like to think there is a secret algorithm that can predict or guarantee admission to an elite school. There isn't. You'll find no shortcuts or "side door" in the college admissions process, even if you think you have the formula figured out. For almost every admissions decision, there are multiple factors that determine the fate of an applicant, most of which do not depend solely on numbers and have shaped an application long before it's ever submitted. While there is no formula per se, there is a playbook or road map that many college counselors and families can use to succeed in the college admissions process, and we would like to share some of it with you.

First of all, let's define success for the college search. We define it as a family and, more specifically, a student having college choices. Success is not tied to being admitted to an elite institution. Success is not associated with having a full scholarship. Success, as we see it, is when a family understands that the life of their student is precious and that they, as a family, have many options to consider. When colleges, plural, are in front of a teenager and their family, and they can choose where they want to go and why, they are successful.

For the better part of the past twenty-five years, we have been deeply committed to college counseling on both the secondary-school side and the university side, helping families and students navigate the college search, application, and admissions journey. Through our combined time spent working in college admissions and enrollment management, it's safe to say that there are few scenarios we have not encountered in assisting thousands of families with different goals and aspirations and in reviewing tens of thousands of applications between the two of us. In our personal and professional experiences, we understand college from the perspectives of both Historically Black Colleges and Universities (HBCUs) and predominantly white institutions (PWIs) and from the viewpoints of first-generation and fourth-generation college graduates. We put this book together to cover the scope of questions that Black families have, with a clear understanding that Black people are not a monolithic group but rather have a variety of experiences and perspectives.

We are Black parents who also happen to be college admissions professionals. We understand many of the unique questions, concerns, and needs of other Black parents approaching the college admissions process. Blacks in the United States have always had challenges in accessing higher education. As Black families, we must think about the spaces we are putting our children in and how they will be supported. We must begin to think as early as elementary school about where they should attend college, to consider public or private schooling if that is an option, and what is the best path for them given their personal, educational, and cultural needs. While these choices are not unique to Black families, they often are difficult to make when they put Black children in predominantly white environments for most of their formative years.

Given the racial history of this country and the current climate of social unrest, Black families, who have always had to ask compelling questions about cultural safety and significance, are increasingly asking, Should my child go to an HBCU or a PWI? In our experience, Black families usually land in one of three camps in their answer: (1) those who believe PWIs are inherently better than HBCUs because they will offer their child a better chance at career success and more closely resemble the "real world"; (2) those with parents who attended an HBCU and want their child to follow in their footsteps and so dismiss the idea of their child attending a PWI; and (3) families who will consider *all* institutions and let the decision be guided by financial aid, location, majors offered, and ultimately what's best for their family situation. While the third camp is probably the largest, the first two make the most noise.

The debate between HBCU and PWI graduates rages on for Black parents of our generation, those who went to college in the 1980s or 1990s. Rarely would an HBCU graduate prefer a PWI for their child, yet some PWI graduates see HBCUs—especially the Black Ivies—as safe havens for their culturally confused and often "white adjacent" children. These are Black children who have gone to elementary, middle, and high school with mostly white students and feel more comfortable with them than with other Black students. The thought of going to an HBCU scares some Black children who do not think of themselves as "down" or as "having a Black card." Some would argue that it's precisely these children who should attend an HBCU to be a part of the rainbow of Black people.

HBCU grads poke their chests out proudly, and many declare that it was the best decision of their lives. They plant seeds of HBCU love in their children at an early age, and some parents unwaveringly predetermine that their child will attend their alma mater or that their money will go only to an HBCU. Tim, for instance, has claimed that his son will go to Morehouse College, even though he has spent three times as many years at Emory University as he did at Morehouse and his children would go to Emory for free if admitted!

We cannot tell you how many times in our work as admissions professionals we have been asked where we went to school. A Black college graduate's answer to that question will attract judgment, regardless of what it is. If you went to an HBCU, there will be those who think your education was inferior to those who attended a PWI. And if you attended a PWI, there will be those who'll question why you made that choice and doubt your knowledge of racial inequalities in America.

If we think about success in financial terms, HBCUs deserve more credit than they receive in mainstream white media. Few billionaires have influenced the world as much as Oprah Winfrey, one of the richest Black people on the globe, who attended Tennessee

State University, an HBCU; or Black billionaire businessman David Steward, who attended the University of Central Missouri, a PWI. However, if you measure success by accomplishments, you could point to President Barack Obama and First Lady Michelle Obama, who attended Columbia University and Princeton University, respectively. The list of successful Black college graduates, from both HBCUs and PWIs, is extensive, and we will highlight many of them throughout the book.

The debate over which type of school is "best" for our children is endless. However, what has become clear to us is that Black students should find the best school of whichever type to nurture their development and identity and feed their academic souls. If choosing a college to attend was as simple as thinking about majors, financial aid, the college's location, and its rate of job placement, we would not be writing this book. We know that there is much more to the decision, and that's why the question about which college type to choose is so complicated to answer. Given the number of times we have heard the question, we have learned to highlight the strengths of both institutional types. But we are also aware of what the family really wants to know—which is better?—and we always end our answer with "it all depends on what the student is looking for." Some families are simply looking for the best school to prepare their student for a postgraduate

Tennessee State University (HBCU)
Nashville, TN
6,000 Undergraduates
Public
Graduate Students: Yes
Setting: Urban

University of Central Missouri (PWI)
Warrensburg, MO
10,000 Undergraduates
Public
Graduate Students: Yes
Setting: Remote

Columbia University (PWI)
New York, NY
6,200 Undergraduates
Private
Graduate Students: Yes
Setting: Urban

Princeton University (PWI)
Princeton, NJ
5,300 Undergraduates
Private
Graduate Students: Yes
Setting: Suburban

Exercise: List the ten most successful (according to your definition of success) Black people, dead or alive, who attended college, and then write next to their name whether they attended an HBCU or a PWI.

career, while other families are thinking about the student's identity and how the college environment will help shape their entire life.

Preparatory Research

For the past two years, as we prepared to write this book, we conducted interviews, facilitated roundtable discussions, and administered surveys to Black parents who expect their children to go to college. Many of the parents went to HBCUs, and others went to PWIs. While we heard a range of opinions on the value of education and how to construct an educational trajectory, there were common themes: safety—mental, emotional, and physical—and preparation for the process. Black families told us they do not feel as informed about the college admissions process as they want to be, and they often blamed the school their child attends. Most were clear that they would not predetermine where their child would go, but many were also aware that the chasm between an HBCU and a PWI experience is wide and they, ultimately, want what's best for their child. One thing that we did find alarming, however, was that of the Black parents we surveyed, 94 percent believe there is a perception that PWIs are superior to HBCUs.

We also spent time with high school college counselors and asked them how Black families are treated in the college preparation process. We asked counselors, mostly white, what HBCUs they were familiar with and if they encourage their Black students to apply. Most were candid and sheepishly admitted that they were not familiar with HBCUs apart from the Black Ivies and that they could do better.

Arrangement of the Book

This book was designed to provide a road map and educational resource for Black families who want to understand the experience of college search and college admissions. To explain it, we arranged the book in three parts. Part I focuses on the *context* of higher education for Black students looking to go to college. There are several variables that will influence the colleges and universities that families consider long before students enter high school. We discuss how parents can think about primary and secondary education, whether an HBCU or a PWI may be the better choice for your child, and what particular institutions will provide the best return on investment and career opportunities for your child, if that is a priority. Before you begin to think about what institutions you will be looking at, we believe it is essential to ask what college can offer your child beyond an education alone. We also think that it's critical to discuss the current higher education landscape as well as other external factors.

Part II focuses on the *X factors* to be considered in college admissions. We begin with what questions you and your family should be asking, examine some of the areas that can cause anxiety and tension in the college search process, and consider gender inequities and other concerns that may require a specific path. We also examine what families should be thinking about if their student is an athlete or artist or has another talent that will guide their college search. Finally, we bring up one of the biggest considerations in the college admissions process: money. How families address these X factors will be critical to identifying schools that will be a good fit for their student.

In part III we focus on the college admissions *process* itself, which begins earlier than most of us want to believe. We address how to make the most out of college visits, how to manage the relationship between a school's college counseling office and your family, and how standardized testing factors in the process. We also get into the nuts and bolts of the college application. We not only provide you with a guide through the process, from start to finish, more importantly we provide the insight and resources you and your family will need to feel confident about applying to college. Following part III, you'll find appendixes and other additional resources.

Things to Keep in Mind as You Read This Book

We have summarized below some of the most important messages of the book.

Guide your child. Their own self-awareness is key, but you, as their parent, also have to steer them in the college admissions process.

Explore different interests, strengths, majors, careers, and colleges. Nothing is more important than being open-minded in the college admissions process. With some four thousand colleges and universities in the United States, there are plenty to choose from.

Encourage self-advocacy. Your child has to step up in the college search. While we want you to be a copilot, your child has to want this more than you want it for them.

Examine the differences between HBCUs and PWIs. Culturally, educationally, and financially, there are elements that need to be fully evaluated.

Execute excellent applications and essays. This is not to be taken lightly. Whether it's for a college or a scholarship, have your child put significant time and effort into preparing the best possible profile that will make them stand out.

Ensure you have choices. College admissions success means having college choices. Then you and your child get to consider what their life plan should be for the next five to ten years.

Free Online Resources

Explore these resources when you begin the college admissions process.

College Search
CollegeXPress.com

Bigfuture.collegeboard.org
Collegedata.com

Financial Aid
FinAid.org
Studentaid.ed.gov
Scholarships.com

Testing
ACT.org
Collegeboard.com
Fairtest.org

General
Commonapp.org
Coalitionforcollegeaccess.org

PART I

Context

CHAPTER 1

Black Parents

The Choices We Make Now Matter Later

Overview

Black parents who are college graduates, especially first-generation college graduates, want our children to have more than we did, and their education is central to that. Many of us believe it is our duty to consider how we achieved our educational success and then take it a step farther with our children. This often means sending our children to private schools or moving to a more affluent suburb in search of better educational options. The goal of these choices is often to expose our children to a more rigorous academic curriculum on their educational trajectory to a good college and beyond.

Along the way, though, we may compromise culture and community. Is this *right*? Is this *good*? How does this affect our children, not just emotionally, but in their chances for college admissions success? And are there other potential consequences to these decisions? This chapter explores how parents' choices at early stages of their child's education affect their college counseling and ultimately their college choices.

Parents ask questions about where and how to educate their children before their children are born. Parents elated to be pregnant start planning everything from their child's baby shower to their wedding. Every parent declares they want what's best for their child and will offer them all the things they themselves did not have and more. Parents often try to replicate all the advantages of their own upbringing, if they had them, that helped them find success. We all do it; it's just the nature of being a parent. There is no one definitive guide to parenting, and each child is different and will experience the world in different ways. We parents are a collection of our personal experiences, and we use those experiences, both good and bad, to help chart a path for our children to succeed in life. A day does not go by when we as parents don't have to make a decision about our children, but the decision-making about our children's education and college preparation should start earlier rather than later. These decisions often aren't made overnight and require hard conversations, resources, and in most instances with Black families, some sense of compromise.

Black parents want for their children what everyone else wants: to be better and to have more. But what does that mean and to what expense or extent? We want our children to lead lives with few regrets, have enriching and rewarding friendships, and, yes, obtain financial assets. We understand that much of the training for success happens in the home and in school as early as elementary. We are committed to putting our children around other children and families that are upwardly mobile and financially rewarded. Many of our choices, especially early on, are about who will care for and teach our children. If we are financially able to, many of us have chosen to live in places where the educational options are good. Public schools serve communities, and the taxpaying populations surrounding these schools expect the schools to elevate their children. Often we Black parents choose an area to live in after we have thoroughly vetted its public schools. Many parents are willing to pay higher property taxes or even rent a house in a school district that they believe will benefit their child. Unfortunately, what frequently happens is that these neighborhoods are not as diverse with other Black people as we would like them to be. The educational resources of affluent white neighborhoods dwarf those of predominantly Black neighborhoods in most cases, and for us to have access to these rich resources, we parents may have to decide to be "the onlys" or one of a few Black families in a whiter, richer community. This is not an easy choice because we are placing our children in predominantly white neighborhoods and schools just to be . . . "better?"

> *"We knew when we moved to our suburban neighborhood 18 years ago that we were moving into a predominantly white area, but we were moving there for the property value and school system. While our son's education has not been without issue, as a Black parent those are just some of the decisions you have to make; you will take 80 percent good and know there is going to be 20 percent bad."*

Given how much college preparation has changed over the last twenty years, we feel it's important to provide Black parents insight into how their educational and school choices can affect the college admissions process.

Where Should I Send My Child to School?

I (Tim) can recall an occasion when I was out with a friend in Atlanta who is an executive at an investment bank. As we were talking, he casually asked me, "What is the best high school for my children to go to?" At that time, I believe, his oldest was twelve. Given his success in his profession, I knew he had asked the question with no concern about money; rather, he wanted to know how best to position his children for success beyond college. Knowing that he lived in Buckhead, an affluent part of Atlanta, I told him to save his money and send his children to North Atlanta High School, a public school, have them enroll in the International Baccalaureate program, and they will be in good stead. He then mentioned some private schools and asked, "Why not them instead?" My response was simple: "Do you want them to get a good education, or do you want to tell your friends they go to private school?" He paused before he responded and then said that he wanted them to go where they will be prepared to succeed at any college. I said North Atlanta was the right place then; it has long been known for its International Bacca-laureate and Advanced Placement programs and the good academic preparation of its students. As Emory University's longtime admissions representative for Atlanta, I knew firsthand that no college that recruits in Atlanta does not make it a priority to stop there for the quality and diversity of the student population. Currently my friend's oldest child is entering her senior year there, and the family is highly satisfied with the educational experience she has had.

I too had to go through this thought process when I considered my own children's education. They spent their toddler years in a Montessori school, and we were very pleased with the education they received. However, with my wife and I having attended public school, we were adamant about them transitioning eventually to a public school. As they approached the age when children begin kindergarten, we thought that would be a great time to execute our plan, but we did not know how complicated it would be. From beginning to end the process took place over six stressful months. In identifying public schools that we felt good about our children going to, we found that they were either in neighborhoods we could not afford, were out in the suburbs where we did not want to live, or did not have the diversity we were looking for. As we continued our search, we knew we were going to have to make some compromises. As for the option of keeping them in their current school, we were finding that the rising cost of the school would not be sustainable for us, and we just had to make a decision. Ultimately, we found a school in a neighborhood we liked that met every criterion we had, but we ended up renting an older, smaller home in the neighborhood to make it work. While it was a small compromise to make in the larger scheme of things, we are somewhat at the mercy of the home's owners. These were the decisions we had to make about our children's elementary school.

My friend and I were fortunate enough to have several choices by living in Atlanta, and he and his family had considerable resources at their disposal. Not all families have as many options, however.

Many parents are presented with choices of public schools that don't have resources comparable to those of private schools. In some cases there are charter school options, but many have no guarantee of admission and often bring additional challenges such as transportation and limited extracurricular options. Parents also have to consider the environment in which their children will be educated. Private schools may have many resources to support students, yet they often lack the diversity that many Black families are looking for. These are the challenges that can shape academic preparation and identity formation.

Just so that we are clear, we are not implying that private schools are better than public or charter schools; we are just acknowledging that in many instances there are trade-offs in the choices we make as parents. Some trade-offs are hard to accept. To put your students in the best possible educational position, you must address these questions in elementary and middle school. The academic preparation students receive in those formative years sets the foundation for their high school courses. In part III, "Process," we provide a lot more context for how the foundation formed in elementary and middle school can impact students' performance in high school courses, their college preparation, and how competitive they will be in college admissions.

> "My children began in a suburban public school, but after a couple of racial incidents with my son we decided to move them to private school. While he was an all-A student in public school, when he moved to private school, his grades dropped. He ended up doing well and enrolling in a good college, but he did not have as many options as we would have liked. At the same time we had some family friends that had kids the same age as ours that left their kids in the public school system that we moved from, and they had several more options than my son did. While I know there are other things at play, I could not help but ask myself, 'Did I do the right thing moving him into a private school?'"

In the table at the end of the chapter we share the model a parent developed to help his family evaluate the pros and cons of moving their child from public to private school. The model gives evidence of how early and to what extent some parents think about their children's education and the factors they consider.

Preparing to Think about College

The question of school choice is one that we all ask at some point as parents because it is more than a choice about education alone; it is also about the development, safety, and well-being of our children. It is critical that Black parents understand that almost everything their child does from middle school through high school influences their college options. Whether it is course selection, standardized testing, assorted activities, or the experiences that students write about in their application essays, Black parents need to be aware that everything matters. The college search and application process does not start in the eleventh grade. It starts with exposure to what college is; the activities and classes that students have in elementary school and middle school may affect their activities and courses in high school. It pains us that too many Black parents depend on what they know from twenty or thirty years ago when they applied and went to college. Much of that is not relevant for what your child will go through. Your children will never wait in line to register for classes, fill out a paper application, and, depending on your situation, may never have to know where the office of financial aid is or have to wait on a refund check.

We want Black parents to be *drivers* of their children's college search and application process. In *Who Gets In and Why: A Year inside College Admissions*, author Jeffrey Selingo defines *drivers* as voracious consumers of information, those who read guidebooks or regularly talk to college counselors or others who can help them, as opposed to *passengers*, who are simply along for the ride through the admissions process. Being a driver means "taking the wheel" and steering your children toward the kinds of schools you think may be best for them given who they are. We want to give you the information to make informed decisions as early as you need to make them so that your child has the educational and life options they want for themselves. This is how other cultural groups are winning in the college application process. They understand that the traditional selection process continues to favor families that focus on advanced high school courses, test scores, and distinctive extracurricular activities. Pop culture would have you believe that "diversity" trumps all in PWI college admissions, whether racial diversity or diversity from first-generation college students. This is simply not true. Many colleges enroll students from a multitude of socioeconomic backgrounds, which is key to achieving diversity in higher education.

However, in a 2021 article in the *Atlantic*, author Caitlin Flanagan revealed that although less than 2 percent of the nation's students attend so-called independent schools (a type of private school), 24 percent of Yale's class of 2024 attended an independent school. At Princeton, that figure is 25 percent. At Brown and Dartmouth, it is even higher, at 29 percent. The numbers are even more astonishing when you consider that the students are not distributed evenly across the country's more than 1,600 independent schools; instead, they are concentrated in the most exclusive ones. The Dalton School in New York City has sent about a third of its graduates to the Ivy League in the past five years. Ditto for the Spence School in New York City. Harvard-Westlake, in Los Angeles, sent forty-five kids to Harvard alone. Noble and Greenough School, in Massachusetts, did

Yale University (PWI)
New Haven, CT
6,792 Undergraduates
Private
Graduate Students: Yes
Setting: Midsize City

Brown University (PWI)
Providence, RI
6,200 Undergraduates
Private
Graduate Students: Yes
Setting: Urban

Dartmouth College (PWI)
Hanover, NH
4,600 Undergraduates
Private
Graduate Students: Yes
Setting: Remote

Harvard University (PWI)
Cambridge, MA
5,200 Undergraduates
Private
Graduate Students: Yes
Setting: Urban

even better: fifty kids went to Harvard. These numbers show that where you send your child to high school can impact where they later go to college.

When we spoke to families before writing this book, many assumed that being Black and having good grades and test scores equals automatic admission to the most selective PWIs. This is not so. What most institutions want is diversity, and that can come in different forms. Offering educational opportunity to historically underrepresented populations is critical to achieving diversity, which may mean that, if your child enjoyed educational and extracurricular opportunities that other applicants did not, your child may be viewed as just another applicant, regardless of their race or ethnicity.

Many assume that PWIs need Black students. No. What most colleges and universities are looking for is diversity, and that comes in many forms. One of the biggest forms of diversity that institutions are looking for is socioeconomic diversity. So while there is a kind of diversity that a Black student can bring to campus, if their mother is a doctor and father is a lawyer and that student attended private school, an admissions officer may wonder whether this student will really bring a different perspective to campus more so than someone from another background who did not have as many opportunities. Thus, depending on your situation, you may think your child will bring diversity to a school, but in fact your child could be looked on as just another privileged applicant.

Another point we need to emphasize is this: if having elite college options is important to you as a parent and you are choosing to impart your values and opinions to your child, *you must start this process early.* It can be lengthy, and having a clear story and high grades and test scores, which may require tutoring, as well as an array of extracurricular activities helps tremendously. If you are the parent of a young child and as yet have no clear idea who your child will be academically, culturally, or what they will like to do, this will be hard to predict. But for those who have a child in late middle school or the early years of high school, knowing who they are and exploring the range of educational opportunities you have will help your child as they take the next steps.

The path to college is a long one, and depending on the college options your family is looking at, you may have to make some important decisions long before you thought you had to. Even if you don't dream of your child going to a top-tier school, the earlier that you as a family begin to think about the process of applying and going to college, the more options you will have available to you. We have found in our experience that there are fewer and fewer "guarantees" nowadays when it comes to college admissions. Some schools that twenty years ago admitted students at a high rate have since become more selective, so you can no longer assume that a school will consider you a legacy or that a school needs Black students. In many instances that is not the case. The process of college preparation needs to start now.

Example of a Pro and Con Analysis of Public versus Independent (Private) School

Panel A. Priorities for Sally's Education

Priority	Description
Education fundamentals	Ensure Sally establishes a firm foundation in reading, math, and writing
In-person instruction	Keep Sally in in-person schooling
COVID safety	COVID protocols must be sufficient to keep us safe within reason
Size & resources	School should not be overlarge and should have resources for plentiful extracurricular activities
Reasonable cost	Must be affordable for us
Diversity	School should expose Sally to diverse backgrounds across the student body, faculty leadership, and curriculum
High school's reputation	School's reputation should position Sally to be competitive in her college applications
Convenience	Ensure Mom has a reasonable and sustainable daily routine to get the children to/from school

Panel B. Scenario 1: Live in Current Home and Compare Local Public School with Independent School

Priority	Weight	Local public school	Score: 1 (con) → 6 (pro)	Independent school	Score: 1 (con) → 6 (pro)
Education fundamentals	0.2	▸ Overall the curriculum is probably on par with the independent school in the primary grades. ▸ Students in Sally's class are behind because of COVID. Teachers will struggle to help performing students advance because they are likely to be preoccupied with struggling students. This dynamic is unlikely to resolve itself in the near term. Additional tutoring will be required for Sally.	3	▸ Presents the opportunity for high-caliber schooling if you are in the advanced track, but the school does track. If you are just taking regular classes, there is limited educational benefit. ▸ Outside tutoring and support will likely be needed to ensure Sally lands in the advanced track. ▸ One of the teachers at the independent school seemed very drab, but there is apparently no way to request the teacher you want.	4
COVID safety / In-person instruction	0.2	▸ School has stronger COVID protocols than the independent school (weekly testing and daily temp checks). ▸ School's track record from last year suggests some risk that the school could close again if the virus gets bad. That said, this year we have vaccines, and the teachers are vaccinated, so a full closure is probably unlikely.	3	▸ School doesn't do daily temp checks or weekly testing. Is very disciplined about masks and social distancing in the classrooms. ▸ School unlikely to close.	4

(continued)

Example of a Pro and Con Analysis of Public versus Independent (Private) School (*continued*)

Priority	Weight	Local public school	Score: 1 (con) → 6 (pro)	Independent school	Score: 1 (con) → 6 (pro)
Size & resources	0.15	▸ School is large overall and perhaps bigger than ideal for Sally. ▸ Has resources but in limited supply. Getting access requires parents to be very proactive and engaged.	4	▸ School is smaller overall and more of an ideal size for Sally and the level of attention/support she often thrives in. ▸ Many more accessible and enriching extra-curricular activities that Sally will enjoy.	6
Reasonable cost	0.15	▸ Free tuition. ▸ Will need to spend dollars on wraparound services; could easily spend $12K/year on these support services; that said, they will be 1-on-1 and won't be subsidizing programs for other folks.	5	▸ $25K/year; coupled with second child's schooling, we'll be spending $50K/year on primary education. From now to graduation, we'd be committing ~$250K-$275K. ▸ If additional 1-on-1 support (tutoring, etc.) is needed to increase probability that Sally lands in the advanced track, that's on top of tuition expense.	1
Diversity	0.1	▸ Very diverse across faculty and leadership. ▸ More middle- / upper-middle-class Brown kids attend school. Sally is likely to have friends across the spectrum of background and experience.	5	▸ Most diverse of similar private schools (in both faculty and student body). ▸ Kids in a similar socioeconomic status at independent school more likely to be white; could jeopardize Sally's self-esteem. ▸ Alumni shared tough stories of how they were treated; the head of school responded with meaningful action.	3

Priority	Weight	Local public school	Score: 1 (con) → 6 (pro)	Independent school	Score: 1 (con) → 6 (pro)
High school's reputation	0.1	▸ Local public school is viewed as a great school by college admissions officers. If Sally is on an equivalent track at local public school, her odds of entry are on par or better than at the independent school.	4	▸ Independent school does not advantage or disadvantage students on college applications. It really will come down to what track Sally ends up on and how she performs. ▸ The independent school's name drives more impact in social circles than in college admissions.	4
Convenience	0.1	▸ 2 min. from the house; she can eventually walk to school. ▸ She gets the benefit of living in the neighborhood with schoolmates.	6	▸ Basically infeasible to get both Sally and her sibling to and from school each day without additional help. ▸ Carpooling adds risk (not comfortable having Sally ride with someone we don't know). ▸ If we move to a different part of the city, the busing option increases convenience considerably.	1
Weighted Total			4.05		3.45

(continued)

Example of a Pro and Con Analysis of Public versus Independent (Private) School (*continued*)

Panel C. Further Considerations

Input from others	S: "If local public school was an option, I probably wouldn't be at the independent school." T: "Independent school is a large school where people go for the name. The education really isn't that different and not worth the price." R: "My kids coming from local public school knew more than the kids from the independent school." [There's a question about what track the kids were on.]
Wildcards	▸ Future moves / neighborhood: If we move, then local public school becomes a lot less convenient, and we may end up in private school. In that scenario, we are better off switching to the independent school now, assuming we can sort out the logistics. At some point in the future, Sally would have to test into the independent school. ▸ Decision speed: Making the decision to switch this quickly feels hasty. What are the consequences of deferring for a year? ▸ Decision correction: If we leave local public school, there is no guarantee that we can get Sally back in.

CHAPTER 2

Shift in Power

The Resurgence of HBCU Culture

Overview

HBCUs have been an integral part of American higher education, given the United States' long history of racism and segregation. For decades, these institutions have been the foundations for Black achievement and excellence—from Thurgood Marshall to Toni Morrison to Langston Hughes. For the most part, conversations about HBCUs were limited in mainstream media following the Civil Rights Act of 1964. While there has always been a segment of the population that has recognized the value and importance of HBCUs, now more than ever they are being featured and celebrated in American popular culture because of the current emphasis on empowering racial differences and a variety of celebrity endorsements. This chapter examines the reasons that HBCUs have seen a resurgence in popularity.

In the words of Todd Smith, better known as LL Cool J, "Don't call it a comeback / I've been here for years." While some people may just now be paying attention to HBCUs, they have been a staple in US higher education since 1837, when Cheyney University in Pennsylvania opened its doors as the first HBCU, although Lincoln University, also in Pennsylvania, claims to be the first degree-granting HBCU after it opened in 1853. This point of contention over primacy has been going on since the schools were founded. Regardless, HBCUs have been a critical means for Black students to obtain a college degree in the United States for almost two hundred years.

Following desegregation, Black colleges continued to serve as the foundation for access to college for Black students, but some of the honor and prestige that historically came from attending these schools began to shift given the new options that became available to Black students. For much of the latter part of the twentieth century, coverage and discussions about HBCUs were limited. However, in the 1980s and 1990s HBCUs made an appearance in popular culture in films like *School Daze* (1988), which provided the world with a glimpse of attending a Black college. At around that same time the world was introduced to what some would argue is the greatest and most influential HBCU of all: Hillman College.

Cheyney University (HBCU)
Cheyney, PA
600 Undergraduates
Public
Graduate Students: Yes
Setting: Suburban

Lincoln University (HBCU)
Lincoln, PA
1,900 Undergraduates
Public
Graduate Students: Yes
Setting: Remote

Although a fictional college that was the setting for the sitcom *A Different World*, Hillman College made an impact on a generation of students. NBC aired the popular show from 1987 to 1993; it opened viewers' eyes to the Black college experience. With a fan base that included graduates from both PWIs and HBCUs, the show framed the idea of the college-going experience for many.

While there are a lot of people and organizations highlighting HBCUs today, no one does it like Vice President Kamala Harris, who is a proud Howard University alumna. She attributes a great deal of her success to the exposure she received to social justice activism, to becoming a member of Alpha Kappa Alpha, and to just being in a place like "Chocolate City" in those formative years.

> "At an HBCU, a young person is shown they can be anything. You step out of the minority and you become the majority. Everything tells you exactly what Aretha told us: You are young, gifted, and Black, you come as you are and leave as you aspire to be."
> (US Vice President Kamala Harris)

Stacey Abrams and Raphael Warnock are political game-changers who attended Spelman and Morehouse, respectively. Not only did they change the political landscape in the state of Georgia, they also helped shape how elections will look moving forward. And then there is Michael Strahan, Super Bowl champion, a perennial Pro Bowl player, and successful entrepreneur, who now wakes up the nation on *Good Morning America* and who graduated from Texas Southern University. While these four individuals make a major impact, the groundswell of HBCUs' resurgence is much larger.

Beyoncé's 2018 Netflix special *Homecoming* paid homage to HBCU culture; Netflix CEO Reed Hastings and his wife, Patty Quillin, have donated millions to HBCUs, as has philanthropist MacKenzie Scott, along with several corporations; the 2021 NBA All-Star Game celebrated and donated millions to HBCUs; Coach Deion Sanders is the head football coach at Jackson State University; and recently basketball great LeBron James arranged to have his logo featured on Florida A&M's basketball jerseys. These are some of the notable people and events that have helped train a spotlight on these storied and necessary institutions.

Currently there are a little more than one hundred HBCUs. This is significantly fewer than there were fifty years ago. According to the United Negro College Fund, HBCUs make up only 3 percent of the country's colleges and universities, yet they enroll 10 percent of all Black students and produce almost 20 percent of all Black college graduates. While this number is impressive, the percentage of Black students who received their degrees from HBCUs prior to desegregation was far larger. These institutions were responsible for granting more than 90 percent of the college degrees earned by Blacks prior to desegregation. HBCUs are still responsible, though, for producing the majority of Black doctors, PhDs, federal judges, attorneys, military officers, and other professionals. With such a long history of success, why are HBCUs often overlooked in favor of PWIs by both families and school counselors in the college admissions process? Some Black families have a hard time seeing

HBCUs as viable options for their children. One college counselor explains:

> "A lot of Black families who did not attend HBCUs or have some kind of connection to an HBCU have a hard time considering them as viable options because they are uncertain if they have the value and appeal in comparison to PWIs." (Private school college counselor)

For the better part of sixty years since desegregation in the United States, there was a shift of high-profile Black talent from HBCUs to PWIs. Today, though, with a lot of attention given to social justice issues and the Black Lives Matter movement, along with growing interest in philanthropic giving to HBCUs, these schools are enjoying a resurgence of the popularity and significance they had in the early 1990s, when many hip-hop artists wore HBCU clothing in their music videos. This deliberate fashion statement was a staple in popular television shows and movies such as *Martin*, *The Cosby Show*, *A Different World*, *Boyz n the Hood*, and *School Daze*. While great producers and filmmakers like John Singleton (University of Southern California) and Spike Lee led the charge in the 1990s, there is a current resurgence led by Florida A&M alumnus William Packer, who has helped reignite this tradition of highlighting HBCUs in television and in cinema with several great movies featuring HBCU graduates Taraji P. Henson (Howard) and Terrence J (North Carolina A&T). Packer became the first Black producer of the Oscars in 2022, the same year Wanda Sykes (Hampton University) was a cohost.

University of Southern California (PWI)
Los Angeles, CA
21,000 Undergraduates
Private
Graduate Students: Yes
Setting: Urban

Florida A&M University (HBCU)
Tallahassee, FL
7,400 Undergraduates
Public
Graduate Students: Yes
Setting: Midsize City

North Carolina A&T State University (HBCU)
Greensboro, NC
11,000 Undergraduates
Public
Graduate Students: Yes
Setting: Midsize City

The Unmasking of Being Black in America

While many would like to think that George Floyd's death in 2020 at the hands of a police officer was an isolated incident, it wasn't. The deaths of Breonna Taylor, Eric Garner, Philando Castile, Daunte Wright, and so many other Black people have brought greater attention to a growing tension in race relations that has been building for years. While police brutality was nothing new, the graphic nature of the video that captured Derek Chauvin casually kneeling on the neck of George Floyd made it very real to all that much needed to be done in support of Black Lives Matter to address the hundreds of years of racial oppression that has affected so many parts of the Black experience in the United States, especially when it comes to economics and education.

From November 2016 through January 2021, America was exposed as being at a cultural crossroads during the reign of a tyrant in the White House who intentionally and blatantly divided our nation more than other presidents in recent memory. The effects of his presidency prompted a showdown of racism to a magnitude that we have not seen in decades in our society. There have been numerous cases of Black students who attend predominantly white high schools taking to social media to document painful incidents of racism they experienced at school. Many of the stories and Instagram pages attracted national news, especially since many of these instances took place at some of the country's top private and independent schools.

"Almost every day at my school the white guys in my class ask me for the n-word pass. I feel offended every time, but I gave in to them because of the pressure. I feel like they won't like me if I don't give it to them. Now they say it to me all the time, more than I hear it from my Black friends in my neighborhood. I regret giving them the pass every day, but that is how the boys at my school are. I regret ever going to my school." (Student at a private school in Atlanta, June 22, 2020)

"One day at lunch I asked one of my white peers to throw my cup away because he was next to the trash can. I joked and said, 'do it if Black Lives Matter.' He then said, 'Black lives don't matter' and proceeded to kick my cup. Everyone around him applauded and laughed at me." (Student at a private school in Washington, DC, September 15, 2020)

"When President Obama was elected, we had a school wide assembly to watch his inauguration. I'll never forget sitting in that pew, watching him put his hand on the Bible, and hearing a guy in my grade next to me say, 'I can't wait until this (n-word) gets assassinated.'" (Student at a private school in Chicago, July 1, 2020)

Given these experiences of isolation and hostility, some students and families that would have never looked at HBCUs are now looking to these schools as places of refuge and acceptance. In addition to high schoolers taking to social media, lots of students on PWI campuses chimed in with their experiences as well, and some of them decided to transfer to HBCUs.

Do It for the Culture

In 2018 Beyoncé was set to headline onstage at Coachella. She had taken time off from her music career while she was pregnant and spending time with her young children. Her long-awaited return to the stage caused a great deal of excitement. Many were expecting her to give an unforgettable performance, but I don't know if anyone was expecting *Homecoming*. It was deeply rooted in HBCU culture; it exuded the feel of HBCU football games and traditions—big band sounds and dance and step teams. Those familiar with HBCU culture were well acquainted with everything about the performance, but to many it was an introduction to football Saturdays at an HBCU. Beyoncé did not attend an HBCU, but her father, Mathew Knowles, attended Fisk University in Tennessee, and her upbringing in Houston was steeped in the HBCU culture of Texas Southern and nearby Prairie View A&M. Beyoncé is the biggest celebrity in the world, and for her to use her platform to showcase HBCUs and their culture, and to include HBCUs in the creative process, helped to elevate these great schools.

While Beyoncé is one of the artists that helped put Houston on the map as it relates to music, fellow Houstonian Megan Jovon Ruth Pete, also known as "Megan Thee Stallion," is doing all she can to keep Houston a focal part of the music world and highlight HBCUs as well. As she has risen to great fame in her hip-hop career, she also wanted to keep a promise to her family that she would finish school. In the winter of 2021, she fulfilled that promise when she graduated from Texas Southern University with a degree in health administration. While it's a great accomplishment for any student to complete their college degree, for a young person with everything to make that commitment goes a long way in promoting the value of a college education. That's "doing it for the culture!"

Just as Beyoncé used her giant platform to shine a light on HBCUs, NBA star Chris Paul, the "official" HBCU ambassador, has used the NBA global stage and social media to champion HBCUs. The 2021 NBA All-Star Game was a collective effort by the association's players to bring attention to social justice efforts, but there is no doubt that Chris Paul's passion for Black colleges has

Fisk University (HBCU)
Nashville, TN
900 Undergraduates
Private
Graduate Students: Yes
Setting: Urban

Texas Southern University (HBCU)
Houston, TX
5,300 Undergraduates
Public
Graduate Students: Yes
Setting: Urban

Prairie View A&M University (HBCU)
Prairie View, TX
8,400 Undergraduates
Public
Graduate Students: Yes
Setting: Remote

Wake Forest University (PWI)
Winston-Salem, NC
5,200 Undergraduates
Private
Graduate Students: Yes
Setting: Midsize City

Virginia Union University (HBCU)
Richmond, VA
1,200 Undergraduates
Private
Graduate Students: Yes
Setting: Midsize City

heightened the attention. Although he attended a PWI, Wake Forest University, Chris Paul has supported HBCUs throughout his life and all-star career. He is a native of North Carolina, which is home to several prominent HBCUs. He often wears clothing featuring the names of HBCUs to nationally televised games, and he wore Support Black Colleges–branded clothing in commercials for State Farm Insurance. In November 2021, he hosted the inaugural Chris Paul Classic, which is a two-day doubleheader with Morehouse College, Virginia Union University, West Virginia State University, and Winston-Salem State University.

Another high-profile athlete who is bringing both his celebrity and talent to promoting HBCUs is Coach Deion "Prime Time" Sanders, who attended Florida State University. His acceptance of the head coach position at Jackson State University in Mississippi brought great attention to the school and its athletic program, but since he has been there, he has made it a point to shake up the college football world. Within two years he has already made a big impact on the talent that has joined the program by attracting some of the nation's top four- and five-star recruits, who in previous recruiting cycles would have considered larger, more well-known programs. This movement of top talent to HBCUs is not limited to football. Other top high school and college athletes have decided to forgo larger athletic programs

West Virginia State University (HBCU)
Institute, WV
3,500 Undergraduates
Public
Graduate Students: Yes
Setting: Suburban

Winston-Salem State University (HBCU)
Winston-Salem, NC
4,700 Undergraduates
Public
Graduate Students: Yes
Setting: Midsize City

Florida State University (PWI)
Tallahassee, FL
30,000 Undergraduates
Public
Graduate Students: Yes
Setting: Midsize City

Jackson State University (HBCU)
Jackson, MS
4,700 Undergraduates
Public
Graduate Students: Yes
Setting: Midsize City

Ohio State University (PWI)
Columbus, OH
54,000 Undergraduates
Public
Graduate Students: Yes
Setting: Urban

for the Black college experience. Sanders's coaching at an HBCU inspired other NFL greats—Eddie George, who attended a PWI, Ohio State University, took the head coach job at Tennessee State University, and former NFL head coach Hue Jackson went to Grambling State University—to lead programs at HBCUs. None of these coaches attended an HBCU, but by using their celebrity to bring attention to HBCUs, they are attracting the notice of prospective students and athletes, as well as major donors and corporate sponsors.

Grambling State University (HBCU)
Grambling, LA
4,500 Undergraduates
Public
Graduate Students: Yes
Setting: Remote

In spring 2022, clothing company Ralph Lauren announced an upcoming limited-edition collection dedicated to Morehouse and Spelman. With designs by a Morehouse alumnus, James Jeter, the collaboration represents another elevation of HBCU culture, and Jeter and Ralph Lauren should be saluted for this endeavor.

A New Culture of Giving

One of the biggest challenges that HBCUs have always faced is a shortage of funding. This is probably the biggest reason for the decrease in the number of HBCUs. Both HBCUs and PWIs suffer from minimal giving from their alumni bases, which means that many schools are dependent on state and federal funds, external generated revenue, research funding, tuition revenue, and gifts from major individual and corporate donors. Consequently, most higher education institutions operate on tight budgets. In 2017, alumni giving accounted for only 26 percent of all educational donations.

Some may wonder why schools do not use their endowments to fund their operations, but the reality is that colleges and universities try to build up their endowments, not pull from them. Endowments are often a source of schools' fiscal strength and prestige. There are some HBCUs with sizable endowments, but most HBCUs' endowments are dwarfed by those of some of the nation's oldest universities. To give a sense of the funding disparity, Harvard's endowment is over $50 billion, whereas the largest HBCU endowment, Howard University's, is just over $700 million, followed by Spelman, which has just under $400 million in its endowment. With these great disparities in institutional resources, financial support for HBCUs is critical. Although hundreds of millions of dollars have poured into a small number of HBCUs in the past couple of years, there are so many more schools that need assistance.

The onset of the COVID-19 pandemic in 2020 produced fiscal challenges for all industries. In higher education, institutions had to conduct classes virtually and were not able to house students on campus or host summer camps, which are both large revenue generators for small institutions. Although the pandemic's effects are still being felt in higher education, there recently were record numbers of major gifts for several HBCUs. These generous gifts helped to reestablish the ambitious missions of HBCUs and provided exposure to some of the lesser-known schools. These gifts also inspired corporations such as Master-Card, Home Depot, Federal Express, Dominion Energy, and others to donate and create programs to support students at HBCUs.

Although these generous gifts were celebrated, many familiar with philanthropy would argue that it was the gift from Robert F. Smith to Morehouse College graduates that was the most impactful. In 2019 he pledged to pay off over $34 million in student loans for the graduating class. Mr. Smith is not a Morehouse alum (he attended Cornell University), but his gift was announced as he spoke at commencement. The story dominated national news for days following. Robert Smith, Reed Hastings (Bowdoin College), Michael R. Bloomberg (Johns Hopkins University),

Cornell University (PWI)
Ithaca, NY
15,000 Undergraduates
Private
Graduate Students: Yes
Setting: Midsize City

Bowdoin College (PWI)
Brunswick, ME
1,800 Undergraduates
Private
Graduate Students: No
Setting: Remote

Johns Hopkins University (PWI)
Baltimore, MD
5,300 Undergraduates
Private
Graduate Students: Yes
Setting: Urban

and MacKenzie Scott (Princeton University) are not the only people who have given to HBCUs, of course. We would be remiss if we did not remark that Oprah has been giving to HBCUs for decades, along with many other organizations and individuals committed to HBCUs and their success led by the United Negro College Fund; however, the size of these recent gifts along with their timing is a major reason for a newfound interest in HBCUs.

In addition to increased private and corporate philanthropy for HBCUs of late, the Biden-Harris administration has allocated more than $5.8 billion to the support of Black colleges. The administration appointed Taraji P. Henson and Chris Paul to its HBCU advisory board. The board is led by Drs. Tony Allen (president of Delaware State) and Glenda Glover (president of Tennessee State). Dr. Dietra Trent was appointed the executive director of the White House's HBCU initiative.

When top national recruits decide to attend Jackson State University or other HBCUs programs over Power Five conferences (SEC, ACC, Big 12, Pac-12, Big Ten), it becomes a big deal and makes national headlines, as does Beyoncé taking the stage at Coachella and Ralph Lauren curating a clothing collection; both are sharing Black college culture and fashion with the world. These events have led to increased recognition and fund-raising from philanthropic leaders and corporations. Given the current cultural climate in the country, along with the challenges that many Black students face in education systems, we highly recommend that all Black parents, HBCU alums or not, educate themselves about the historical and current relevance of HBCUs and then encourage their children to consider them to be valuable and viable educational options.

CHAPTER 3

The Power 3
(The Black Ivies)

Overview

There is a best, a top tier, an elite in all industries and professions. HBCUs are no different, and for decades three schools have been leaders in the world of HBCUs. Howard, Spelman, and Morehouse are undeniably the most famous HBCUs, given their long lists of famous alumni and the thousands of other graduates who are committed to serving the world and praising these proud institutions. There are those who attended other great HBCUs (insert the name of your HBCU here: _____) who will take issue with this assertion; however, this chapter is not meant as a slight to any of those other institutions.

This chapter serves as an introduction to the greatness of HBCUs, with Spelman, Howard, and Morehouse serving as proxies for the many other great ones around the country. Just as most people declare that PWIs have a top three with Harvard, Princeton, and Yale, the same argument can be made for these three HBCUs. While some will not agree with this chapter's title, the goal of the chapter is to move the conversation beyond these three schools for Black families looking for great schools and for guidance counselors looking for recommendations among the more than one hundred HBCUs.

———

The argument over who or what is the best happens in social spaces throughout society. Among Black people it happens in beauty salons and barbershops, over spades games and at family reunions and cookouts, on any number of subjects. If you want to get a heated conversation going, just ask a question that begins, "What/Who is the best . . . ?" While many of these conversations are highly subjective, in most instances there is some agreement about the top picks in whatever category you are discussing. For instance, if someone were to ask who is the best basketball player of all time, for which there is no real argument in our opinion, we would say Michael Jordan (University of North Carolina, Chapel Hill), but there are others who would say LeBron James, Magic Johnson (Michigan State University), Kareem Abdul-Jabbar (University of California, Los Angeles), or maybe Wilt Chamberlain (University of Kansas). Still, the list is short when talking about the best. Similarly, if someone were to ask about the top Black movies, you would hear titles like *Love Jones*, *The Color Purple*, and *Coming to America* but would likely not hear *Soul Plane*. As hard as it may be to acknowledge, some hierarchies shape the lens through which we see life. Hierarchy is certainly one of the biggest concerns in the college admissions process. Many people focus on the rankings of about one hundred colleges and universities, when in fact there are some four thousand colleges and universities across the country.

University of North Carolina (PWI)
Chapel Hill, NC
18,000 Undergraduates
Public
Graduate Students: Yes
Setting: Midsize City

Michigan State University (PWI)
Lansing, MI
35,000 Undergraduates
Public
Graduate Students: Yes
Setting: Midsize City

University of California at Los Angeles (PWI)
Los Angeles, CA
30,000 Undergraduates
Public
Graduate Students: Yes
Setting: Urban

University of Kansas (PWI)
Lawrence, KS
35,000 Undergraduates
Public
Graduate Students: Yes
Setting: Midsize City

As we wrote this book, we reflected on the many names in Black America that serve as the standards of inspiration and leadership; the names that immediately came to mind were Congressman John Lewis, Vice President Kamala Harris, Dr. Martin Luther King Jr., Reverend Jesse Jackson, President Barack Obama, and Justice Thurgood Marshall—all with the exception of President Obama were graduates of HBCUs. While there are Black success stories and graduates from all higher education institutions, many of the names that defined Black success in the twentieth century and are defining success in the twenty-first century are HBCU graduates, and most of them had some direct or indirect connection to Howard, Morehouse, or Spelman.

Should these three schools be the only HBCUs your child considers? Do they have everything your child needs? Is our statement about prestige unfair to other HBCUs and their history and efforts?

Howard, Morehouse, and Spelman arguably have the greatest sets of distinguished alumni of any schools in the country, Black or white. Of course, there are other HBCUs with distinguished alumni such as Tennessee State, where Oprah Winfrey went; Lincoln University, where Langston Hughes attended; and Grambling State, where Doug Williams went and later became the first Black quarterback to win the Super Bowl, just to name a few.

Spelman

In many college rankings, there is no HBCU ranked higher than Spelman College. Spelman has secured its position as the top HBCU in the country for years. And if you meet a Spelman graduate, she will surely tell you why or be "undaunted" by you not agreeing. Since its founding in 1881, Spelman has been the leader in educating Black women to accomplish great things and to commit their lives to service. As a liberal arts school, much like its brother school Morehouse, Spelman's primary aim is to prepare its graduates to be leaders in their chosen vocation. There is an expectation that Spelman women will shine their light on the world and boldly claim that their alma mater is part of the reason they are so powerful.

If you are looking for a name that speaks to the best of Spelman, you need look no farther than political powerhouse Stacey Abrams, class of 1995. Her grassroots organization Fair Fight created voter awareness and fought voter suppression leading up to the 2020 election, and it provided a network to change the senate makeup in Georgia. Spelman's place among the top HBCUs is not due solely to its name recognition but also to its track record for producing top doctors, lawyers, and leaders in all industries. Its list of graduates includes Rosalind Brewer, who is currently serving as the CEO of Walgreens and is one of only two Black women serving as the CEO of Fortune 500 companies. Prior to taking her leadership role at Walgreens, Brewer served as the COO of Starbucks. The other is Thasunda Brown Duckett, the CEO of TIAA, who attended the University of Houston.

University of Houston (PWI)
Houston, TX
38,000 Undergraduates
Public
Graduate Students: Yes
Setting: Urban

The recently coined "Black Girl Magic" names a movement where Black women empower other Black women and see one another as supportive and inspirational. As Black people, our children need to be pushed to excellence, first by us and then by their peers. This happens at Spelman, and it's why every brilliant Black girl needs to learn more about Spelman before she makes a college decision. Spelman will not be for everyone, but given its history of producing some of the most accomplished Black women ever in the arts, medicine, business, academics, and politics, why wouldn't you consider it? Many Spelman women tell stories of their other college options, including admission to Ivy League schools. They made the decision not to attend these other schools because they wanted an HBCU experience, had concerns about the social environment of a PWI, or wanted to be surrounded by the power of other Black women. Clearly, Spelman women are in a class by themselves.

It is hard for us as Black men to rank one school over another if they are all serving Black people well, but we know there are hierarchies with "better" and "best." Spelman is the best, has produced the best, and expects to be the best. Your daughter must be a superlative student to get into Spelman and have access to its exclusive community. The school admits less than 40 percent of its applicants and expects them to have a grade point average (GPA) above 3.8, an SAT score above 1200, and a score between 27 and 30 on the ACT. And that is just to start. Young women must also have demonstrated a commitment to service and have established themselves as leaders who want to contribute to society. High school students who want to attend Spelman are usually near the top of their graduating class, have taken advanced coursework (Advanced Placement or International Baccalaureate courses), have extensive extracurricular activities, and have written a personal essay that reveals what's most important to them about the next stage of their educational journey. Simply put, applicants to Spelman need to work before they play, understanding that their social life comes secondary to their scholarly aspirations.

Morehouse

Morehouse stands alone as the premier all-men's HBCU, not only because it's the only one, but also because of the kinds of young men it attracts and nurtures. Morehouse men are intent on their goals. College is not a playground but rather is the first step of their life's ascension. As we discuss in chapter 8, we understand that college-educated Black men are, unfortunately, an endangered species. For multiple reasons, we are a serious minority on PWI campuses and on co-ed HBCU campuses as well. A recent statistic cited for most HBCU campuses is a ratio of women to men of seven to one. The Atlanta University Center, which consists of Morehouse, Spelman, and Clark Atlanta University, has a male to female ratio of nine to one. This suggests that Black men have not been given the same educational foundation or have not taken as much advantage of educational opportunities as others have; thus they need a place dedicated to their development. Morehouse is that place.

When it comes to Morehouse, the name of one of its graduates must be mentioned: Dr. Martin Luther King Jr. His legacy as a scholar and civil rights leader has helped define how the world sees Morehouse and has helped shape many graduates who walk in his footsteps, such as Raphael Warnock, class of 1991, who is currently serving in the US Senate. Like Dr. King, he too served as a minister at Ebenezer Baptist Church. While Dr. King is the gold standard of Morehouse graduates, Morehouse College has no shortage of impressive alumni, including Olympic gold medalist Edwin Moses, Academy Award winners Samuel L. Jackson and Spike Lee, civil rights leader Julian Bond, late businessman Herman Cain, and Congressman Cedric Richmond, who is currently serving as a senior advisor in the Biden administration. These accomplished alumni exemplify Morehouse's long track record of graduating leaders across all fields. These alumni have inspired a new generation of Morehouse leaders: Randall Woodfin, mayor of Birmingham, Alabama, who was elected to his second term; and Steven Reed, mayor of Montgomery, Alabama, who is the first African American to hold that position, just to name a few.

Founded in 1867, Morehouse started as and still is the largest all-men's liberal arts college in the country. With only 2,100 men on campus, it prides itself on community, professionalism, and social justice. Legions of men attribute their success and how they approach life to their Morehouse education. It stands alone as *the* college where men are formed for service. Much like Spelman, admission is competitive. Only about six hundred matriculate every year. The expected GPA of an applicant to Morehouse is 3.5, with scores of 1000 on the SAT and between 20 and 25 on the ACT. These might not be earth-shattering statistics for Black students who expect to go to Harvard, Princeton, or Yale, but they are more than solid and are a testament to Morehouse not being measured by whom it admits but by whom it graduates. Men of distinction. Men of character. Men of courage. Morehouse men set themselves apart by understanding that they represent more than just themselves; they also represent their families and the history of their institution. If you have a Black male child whom you wish to make an impact on the world, please consider Morehouse.

The combination of "Spelhouse" is a powerful network of Black excellence. It truly is a family where people understand and appreciate one another. For your child even to consider one of these schools is a privilege, and to attend would be an honor.

Howard

Howard University is called "The Mecca" for a reason. There is a spiritual, euphoric element about being on the campus where so much Black excellence began its journey. While we have already listed the names of its graduates that most Americans know, there are others: award-winning author Ta-Nehisi Coates, former mayor and US ambassador Andrew Young, attorney and the late businessman Vernon Jordan, and Kamilah Forbes, executive producer of the Apollo Theater and an acclaimed filmmaker. These illustrious graduates prove that Howard has and continues to influence all aspects of art, politics, and American culture.

Why is Howard so highly regarded? It's because of its history, location, academic resources, professional schools, and homecoming. In almost every ranking among well-traveled Black folks who have gone to homecomings, Howard is declared to have *the* best homecoming celebration of any HBCU. (*I, Tim, don't agree, but carry on.*)

We're not here to argue or compare, so instead let us simply share why your child should aspire to be a Howard Bison. If your child has gifts in science and is considering medical school, Howard prepares students well. What about business? Howard has a business school dedicated to the study of finance, marketing, and accounting. Does your child want to study communications and aspires to be a journalist or to work in public relations? Howard has that too. And if your child aspires to go into public service or law, Howard has established itself as one of the best.

The beauty of Howard is that there is something for everyone, and we have not even mentioned its recently renamed Chadwick Boseman School of Fine Arts, where dancer and actress Debbie

Allen excelled and where her equally accomplished sister, Phylicia Rashad, is now the dean of the school. Other notable artists that attended Howard are Zora Neale Hurston, Donny Hathaway, Eric Roberson, Taraji P. Henson, Susan Kelechi Watson, and Sean "Diddy" Combs. Nestled in northwest Washington, DC, Howard plays a special role in the politics of the US government. Its proximity to power makes it an ideal place for internships.

To be admitted to Howard, your child must be a scholar. Howard accepts less than 30 percent of applicants, and its GPA and ACT and SAT expectations are higher than Morehouse's and Spelman's. Howard looks for students who are ready to excel in specific disciplines; hence it has the specialized schools of a research university as opposed to being a liberal arts college.

Beyond Spelman, Morehouse, and Howard being household names, they also have what real estate developers value most: location, location. When you think of cities with a history of Black cultural relevance, Atlanta and Washington, DC, are at the top of the list. The foundation of the civil rights movement was formed in Atlanta, and some of the greatest gatherings of Blacks occurred in the District of Columbia: March on Washington, Million Man March, and the inauguration of Barack Obama. Both of these cities have witnessed Black success in so many ways, which makes them great destinations for college and opportunity. In addition to opportunities for internships and conducting research, these locations provide great access to social activities and public transportation. Students can explore and enjoy these great cities as a complement to their college education.

I (Tim) would add that these cities and schools offer what some would call a "safe" space. While many will maintain that there are very few safe spaces for Blacks in this country, HBCUs might be the ideal location for Black students to have their college experience. As an HBCU graduate, I have often wondered why so many Black students apply only to PWIs and then arrive on campus and want more faculty of color, support systems for underrepresented students, and more diversity. But when asked why they did not apply to an HBCU, they say that they or their parents never considered it. I often ask myself why we as Blacks are so insistent on putting ourselves in spaces that are not made for us. Why should we have to alter who we are and how we conduct ourselves to fit in? We have the safe spaces of Morehouse, Spelman, Howard, and other HBCUs that allow us just to be, places where we are surrounded by people who resemble us and nurture us inside and outside the classroom. Our safety and the uplifting of our culture should be a priority for us regardless of whether we favor PWIs or HBCUs.

We profiled Spelman, Morehouse, and Howard to start a conversation about Black colleges, not to put them above other HBCUs. We drew a parallel to Harvard, Princeton, and Yale, which many consider the top PWIs for many of the same reasons we have put forth. People will always want to know what or who is the best; it is just human nature,

Hampton University (HBCU)
Hampton, VA
3,100 Undergraduates
Private
Graduate Students: Yes
Setting: Midsize City

Morgan State University (HBCU)
Baltimore, MD
6,300 Undergraduates
Public
Graduate Students: Yes
Setting: Urban

Xavier University of Louisiana (HBCU)
New Orleans, LA
2,500 Undergraduates
Private
Graduate Students: Yes
Setting: Urban

and we happen to be talking about colleges. Beyond Howard, Morehouse, and Spelman, there are other great HBCUs like Florida A&M, Hampton, North Carolina A&T, Morgan State, Fisk, and Xavier University of Louisiana, which all have histories of producing leaders in all professions. (Please, alums from the other ninety-plus HBCUs, don't come for us!)

Accredited HBCUs by State

Name	State	Type	Campus setting	Campus housing	Undergraduate students
Alabama A&M University	Alabama	4-year, public	Midsize city	Yes	5,093
Alabama State University	Alabama	4-year, public	Midsize city	Yes	3,614
Bishop State Community College	Alabama	2-year, public	Midsize city	No	2,176
Gadsden State Community College	Alabama	2-year, public	Small city	Yes	3,993
H. Councill Trenholm State Community College	Alabama	2-year, public	Midsize city	No	1,526
J. F. Drake State Community and Technical College	Alabama	2-year, public	Midsize city	No	825
Lawson State Community College	Alabama	2-year, public	Midsize city	Yes	2,823
Miles College	Alabama	4-year, private nonprofit	Small suburb	Yes	1,440
Oakwood University	Alabama	4-year, private nonprofit	Midsize city	Yes	1,339
Shelton State Community College	Alabama	2-year, public	Midsize city	No	3,743
Stillman College	Alabama	4-year, private nonprofit	Midsize city	Yes	712
Talladega College	Alabama	4-year, private nonprofit	Remote town	Yes	1,142

(continued)

Accredited HBCUs by State (*continued*)

Name	State	Type	Campus setting	Campus housing	Undergraduate students
Tuskegee University	Alabama	4-year, private nonprofit	Remote town	Yes	2,280
Arkansas Baptist College	Arkansas	4-year, primarily associate's degrees, private nonprofit	Midsize city	Yes	468
Philander Smith College	Arkansas	4-year, private nonprofit	Midsize city	Yes	799
Shorter College	Arkansas	2-year, private nonprofit	Small city	No	223
University of Arkansas at Pine Bluff	Arkansas	4-year, public	Small city	Yes	2,507
Delaware State University	Delaware	4-year, public	Small city	Yes	4,131
Bethune-Cookman University	Florida	4-year, private nonprofit	Small city	Yes	2,746
Edward Waters College	Florida	4-year, private nonprofit	Large city	Yes	2,273
Florida A&M University	Florida	4-year, public	Midsize city	Yes	7,402
Florida Memorial University	Florida	4-year, private nonprofit	Large suburb	Yes	887
Albany State University	Georgia	4-year, public	Small city	Yes	6,102
Clark Atlanta University	Georgia	4-year, private nonprofit	Large city	Yes	3,096
Fort Valley State University	Georgia	4-year, public	Remote town	Yes	2,794

Name	State	Type	Campus setting	Campus housing	Undergraduate students
Interdenominational Theological Center	Georgia	4-year, private nonprofit	Large city	Yes	None; graduate school
Morehouse College	Georgia	4-year, private nonprofit	Large city	Yes	2,152
Morehouse School of Medicine	Georgia	4-year, private nonprofit	Large city	No	None; graduate school
Paine College	Georgia	4-year, private nonprofit	Midsize city	Yes	189
Savannah State University	Georgia	4-year, public	Midsize city	Yes	3,245
Spelman College	Georgia	4-year, private nonprofit	Large city	Yes	2,207
Kentucky State University	Kentucky	4-year, public	Remote town	Yes	2,148
Simmons College of Kentucky	Kentucky	4-year, private nonprofit	Large city	No	140
Dillard University	Louisiana	4-year, private nonprofit	Large city	Yes	1,215
Grambling State University	Louisiana	4-year, public	Remote town	Yes	4,511
Southern University and A&M College	Louisiana	4-year, public	Midsize city	Yes	6,145
Southern University at New Orleans	Louisiana	4-year, public	Large city	Yes	1,941
Southern University at Shreveport	Louisiana	2-year, public	Midsize city	Yes	3,013

(continued)

Accredited HBCUs by State (*continued*)

Name	State	Type	Campus setting	Campus housing	Undergraduate students
Southern University Law Center	Louisiana	4-year, public	Midsize city	No	None; graduate school
Xavier University of Louisiana	Louisiana	4-year, private nonprofit	Large city	Yes	2,517
Bowie State University	Maryland	4-year, public	Large suburb	Yes	5,354
Coppin State University	Maryland	4-year, public	Large city	Yes	2,108
Morgan State University	Maryland	4-year, public	Large city	Yes	6,270
University of Maryland Eastern Shore	Maryland	4-year, public	Remote town	Yes	2,069
Alcorn State University	Mississippi	4-year, public	Remote town	Yes	2,729
Coahoma Community College	Mississippi	2-year, public	Remote town	Yes	1,612
Jackson State University	Mississippi	4-year, public	Midsize city	Yes	4,668
Mississippi Valley State University	Mississippi	4-year, public	Remote town	Yes	1,694
Rust College	Mississippi	4-year, private nonprofit	Remote town	Yes	623
Tougaloo College	Mississippi	4-year, private nonprofit	Midsize city	Yes	762
Harris-Stowe State University	Missouri	4-year, public	Large city	Yes	1,400

Name	State	Type	Campus setting	Campus housing	Undergraduate students
Lincoln University of Missouri	Missouri	4-year, public	Small city	Yes	1,892
Bennett College	North Carolina	4-year, private nonprofit	Midsize city	Yes	232
Elizabeth City State University	North Carolina	4-year, public	Remote town	Yes	1,910
Fayetteville State University	North Carolina	4-year, public	Midsize city	Yes	5,661
Johnson C. Smith University	North Carolina	4-year, private nonprofit	Large city	Yes	1,253
Livingstone College	North Carolina	4-year, private nonprofit	Midsize suburb	Yes	845
North Carolina A&T State University	North Carolina	4-year, public	Midsize city	Yes	11,130
North Carolina Central University	North Carolina	4-year, public	Midsize city	Yes	6,067
Saint Augustine's University	North Carolina	4-year, private nonprofit	Large city	Yes	1,110
Shaw University	North Carolina	4-year, private nonprofit	Large city	Yes	1,152
Winston-Salem State University	North Carolina	4-year, public	Midsize city	Yes	4,689
Central State University	Ohio	4-year, public	Remote town	Yes	4,021
Wilberforce University	Ohio	4-year, private nonprofit	Remote town	Yes	439
Langston University	Oklahoma	4-year, public	Remote town	Yes	1,894

(continued)

Accredited HBCUs by State (*continued*)

Name	State	Type	Campus setting	Campus housing	Undergraduate students
Cheyney University of Pennsylvania	Pennsylvania	4-year, public	Small suburb	Yes	623
Lincoln University	Pennsylvania	4-year, public	Remote town	Yes	1,895
Allen University	South Carolina	4-year, private nonprofit	Midsize city	Yes	656
Benedict College	South Carolina	4-year, private nonprofit	Midsize city	Yes	1,724
Claflin University	South Carolina	4-year, private nonprofit	Remote town	Yes	1,969
Clinton College	South Carolina	4-year, primarily associate's degrees, private nonprofit	Small city	Yes	119
Denmark Technical College	South Carolina	2-year, public	Remote town	Yes	491
Morris College	South Carolina	4-year, private nonprofit	Small city	Yes	395
South Carolina State University	South Carolina	4-year, public	Remote town	Yes	2,020
Voorhees College	South Carolina	4-year, private nonprofit	Remote town	Yes	368
American Baptist College	Tennessee	4-year, private nonprofit	Large city	Yes	55
Fisk University	Tennessee	4-year, private nonprofit	Large city	Yes	879
Lane College	Tennessee	4-year, private nonprofit	Small city	Yes	1,095
LeMoyne-Owen College	Tennessee	4-year, private nonprofit	Large city	Yes	654

Name	State	Type	Campus setting	Campus housing	Undergraduate students
Meharry Medical College	Tennessee	4-year, private nonprofit	Large city	Yes	None; graduate school
Tennessee State University	Tennessee	4-year, public	Large city	Yes	6,000
Huston-Tillotson University	Texas	4-year, private nonprofit	Large city	Yes	1,045
Jarvis Christian College	Texas	4-year, private nonprofit	Remote town	Yes	719
Paul Quinn College	Texas	4-year, private nonprofit	Large city	Yes	468
Prairie View A&M University	Texas	4-year, public	Remote town	Yes	8,372
Southwestern Christian College	Texas	4-year, primarily associate's degrees, private nonprofit	Remote town	Yes	84
St. Philip's College	Texas	2-year, public	Large city	No	12,696
Texas College	Texas	4-year, private nonprofit	Midsize city	Yes	764
Texas Southern University	Texas	4-year, public	Large city	Yes	5,298
Wiley College	Texas	4-year, private nonprofit	Remote town	Yes	615
Hampton University	Virginia	4-year, private nonprofit	Midsize city	Yes	3,063
Norfolk State University	Virginia	4-year, public	Midsize city	Yes	4,992

(continued)

Accredited HBCUs by State (*continued*)

Name	State	Type	Campus setting	Campus housing	Undergraduate students
Virginia State University	Virginia	4-year, public	Small city	Yes	3,659
Virginia Union University	Virginia	4-year, private nonprofit	Midsize city	Yes	1,209
Virginia University of Lynchburg	Virginia	4-year, primarily associate's degrees, private nonprofit	Small city	Yes	122
University of the Virgin Islands	Virgin Islands	4-year, public	Remote town	Yes	1,587
University of the Virgin Islands–Albert A. Sheen Campus	Virgin Islands	4-year, public	Remote town	Yes	546
Howard University	Washington, DC	4-year, private nonprofit	Large city	Yes	7,857
University of the District of Columbia	Washington, DC	4-year, public	Large city	No	3,385
University of the District of Columbia David A. Clarke School of Law	Washington, DC	4-year, public	Large city	No	None; graduate school
Bluefield State College	West Virginia	4-year, public	Remote town	No	1,243
West Virginia State University	West Virginia	4-year, public	Small suburb	Yes	3,502

CHAPTER 4

What Is a Liberal Arts Education, and Is It Worth It?

Overview

In this chapter, I (Shereem) will share my opinions about liberal arts education and how it prepares some people for anything and others for nothing. I ask: Is it worth it for our Black children? Too often I have seen students who were liberal arts majors struggle after graduation to find salaried jobs with high earning potential. This is where my primary frustration lies: In a world that equates success with money, are we doing ourselves and our children a disservice by not steering them toward an education that can lead to wealth generation?

In an ever-changing world, college degrees are no longer regarded as gateways to becoming middle or upper class as they once were. I'm sure some of us know someone who is frustrated with their profession and tends to blame it on their choice of major in college. Even more of us know someone who is not using their degree to its maximum potential. Many of us are still dancing with Sallie Mae, and we ask ourselves, "Was it worth it? Would I be farther ahead in life and wealth building if I were not saddled with educational debt?" And how many of us are in careers that are actually related to our college major?

Many college graduates, of all races, who majored in liberal arts question the monetary or professional value of their degrees. I, Shereem, am one of these people. Degrees in English, sociology, psychology, history, and the like are often undervalued, and in a global economy, without a graduate degree, some undergraduate degrees make many corporate employers question a person's capabilities. Worse than that, many liberal arts degrees suggest that graduates are not qualified to do anything with notable or predictable immediate earning power. There are exceptions, of course, and many of us are creative or entrepreneurial, which means that we may not have needed the degree.

As a liberal arts major (English and African American studies), I often found myself to be selectively employable and never for high-paying jobs that offered bonuses. As I have now witnessed a generation of my peers and mentored many students who have gone on to college, I think that college graduates with preprofessional degrees in business, engineering, computer science, nursing, information systems, architecture, communications, or other fields who are hired right out of college tend to fare better in the long term. Not having career and life direction stalls progress. I do not want this for my children or for yours.

What Is a Liberal Arts Education?

As defined by the Association of American Colleges and Universities, *liberal education* is an approach to undergraduate education that promotes the integration of learning across the curriculum and co-curriculum, and between academic and experiential learning, to develop specific learning outcomes that are essential for work, citizenship, and life. The *liberal arts* are a particular set of disciplines (the humanities, the arts, and the natural and social sciences). A *liberal arts college* is a type of higher education institution whose curriculum is designed to provide a liberal arts education. A liberal education includes the study of the liberal arts and is the approach undertaken at most liberal arts colleges, but it is not exclusive to those disciplines or to that institutional type.

Similarly, as defined by Princeton University—the alma mater of former First Lady Michelle Obama, Amazon's Jeff Bezos, and former

CEO of BET, Bob Johnson—a liberal arts education offers an expansive intellectual grounding in all kinds of humanistic inquiry by having students explore issues, ideas, and methods across the humanities and the arts, and the natural and social sciences. These skills elevate conversations in the classroom and strengthen social and cultural analysis. They also let graduates navigate the world's most complex issues.

A liberal arts education challenges students to consider how to solve problems and trains them to determine which problems to solve and why, preparing them for positions of leadership and a life of service to the nation and all of humanity. Ultimately, a liberal arts education aims to help students "think outside the box."

Think about what?

Morehouse College is a liberal arts college just as Wesleyan University is a liberal arts university. These are the schools that Tim and I attended. Now here's the difference: beyond just teaching students how to think, Morehouse has a business major, a communication major, and specialty engineering majors. These are practical majors that lead to profitable careers. If college is supposed to educate as well as prepare our young people for professional success, we must commit to making sure that our Black children know how to earn money once they graduate. Most of us—Black people—do not come from generational wealth. Thinking about how to get money or hoping to get money has kept too many Black people in economic despair. Sure, we're all waiting for the reparations they owe us for our ancestors, but in the meantime, for us, college is often seen as the first step toward a career and wealth building.

Wesleyan University (PWI)
Middletown, CT
3,000 Undergraduates
Private
Graduate Students: Yes
Setting: Remote

This is why I say *liberal arts is a luxury*. It's nice to learn how to think. It's nice to read books across multiple disciplines that encourage introspection and offer insights into other cultures, literatures, philosophies, and histories. It's advantageous to solve equations and collaborate with classmates on projects. So, I'm all for liberal arts if you can afford it. What I mean is that if you have no assurance that your child will get a job after graduation or has the ability to launch their own venture, they will probably need to go to graduate school to compete. So, I ask, who wants to pay for that? You? Or more loans?

I am a first-generation college student, and my father drove a UPS truck, making deliveries to get me through school. With his "good job" he was able to retire at fifty-five with a healthy pension. Because he had sent me to college, he assumed that I had learned how to invest and make money. Despite my being a teacher at the time, and his knowing I had an English degree, he once said to me, "Since you went to college, I want you to tell me where I should invest my money."

I had no clue what to tell him, and I was disappointed that I didn't know. I was never taught. Maybe he was supposed to teach me; maybe I was supposed to learn in high school or college. What I learned in that moment was that I had to teach myself. But I understood his assumption, and I think it's one we should all consider as Black parents: Is the point of college to get a diploma? Is it to expand our network and knowledge of the world? Is it a training ground to cultivate the capacity to make, keep, and grow money? Too often we think that all three are mutually exclusive, when, in fact, college ideally serves all the above.

The racial wealth gap is a long-standing issue that has plagued America for generations. Research shows that African Americans hold only 4 percent of the country's wealth, and the net worth of a white family is nearly ten times greater than that of a Black family. Aware of these staggering statistics, businessman and philanthropist Robert Smith—who pledged to pay all the student loan debt for the Morehouse class of 2019—and others are doing what they can to break down socioeconomic barriers standing in the way of Blacks generating wealth.

In our many interviews and roundtable discussions, we broached the topic of parents being supportive of their child choosing a liberal arts major that did not equip them to be employable at a satisfactory or predictable salary upon graduation. Most Black parents were clear that they want to and will support their children's choice of major. No one said that they were steering their children only toward making money. When I asked "why not?" the responses were not clear. Some did not want their child to feel pressured; others were convinced that money would come when the time is right. I agree with both sentiments. The harder issue is the accumulation of student and parent debt. With the cost of college being what it is today, how many of us are discussing how this education will be financed and by whom? How will the debt be repaid? My call to action is for us to discuss a plan with our children—for their majors, their possible careers, and, if necessary, their debt repayment.

> "I do not want my child to be burdened with college loans long after graduation. One of the biggest mistakes I made was not having a steady income after college and repaying my loans immediately. I worked as a temp before I decided to go back for my master's because I was never a salaried employee. My undergraduate degree in psychology pretty much demanded that I go back to school, but now I had loans from undergrad and graduate school. I enjoyed studying psychology, and I have no regrets about my choice of major, but I do not want my son to have to struggle after college the way I did. I'm forty-three and still paying off my loans." (PWI graduate and parent)

Some of us exasperate our children by insisting they major in business or STEM (science, technology, engineering, and mathematics). We do it because we don't want them to struggle. We also do it because we want them to be part of a global community that primarily communicates through three ways: money, technology, and art. Remember that Jay-Z line from "Can't Knock the Hustle"? "All Blacks got is sports and entertainment." I remember hearing that line and cringing. I'm sure corporate business moguls Dick Parsons

(University of Hawai'i at Mānoa), Kenneth Chenault (Bowdoin College), and others did too. But the truth hurts, and there is definitely brutal honesty in what Hov said. At the time, Bill Cosby (Temple University), Bob Johnson, L. A. Reid, Eddie Murphy, Michael Jordan, and Oprah Winfrey were the richest Black people that most of us knew. Sports and entertainment. Today, our most recognizable figures are LeBron James, Drake, Kevin Hart, Byron Allen (University of Southern California), Shonda Rhimes (Dartmouth College), and Serena Williams. Again, sports and entertainment. Beyoncé Knowles-Carter and Shawn Carter are known to be American royalty, and their success comes from . . . you already know. Thankfully the Obamas came along and made an exception to the rule, but the norm remains: to be Black and become rich in America, you usually have to start by singing, dancing, making jokes, or running fast. This topic is examined in depth in author Michael Eric Dyson's (Princeton University) most recent book, *Entertaining Race: Performing Blackness in America.*

I hate this norm, but it's real. I wish the Black liberal arts creators involved with AfroTech got more shine. I wish serial entrepreneur Morgan DeBaun, who attended Washington University in St. Louis, was more visible and celebrated. As the founder and CEO of Blavity Inc., she is a media mogul who is not only making Black history; she's making Black present. And she has a liberal arts degree in political science and . . . wait for it . . . entrepreneurship! Ms. DeBaun is a wonderful exception and speaks to my declaration that, with a liberal arts degree, your child may be able to do anything. Similarly, there's Tristan

University of Hawai'i at Mānoa (PWI)
Honolulu, HI
13,000 Undergraduates
Public
Graduate Students: Yes
Setting: Urban

Temple University (PWI)
Philadelphia, PA
26,000 Undergraduates
Private
Graduate Students: Yes
Setting: Urban

Washington University in St. Louis (PWI)
St. Louis, MO
7,600 Undergraduates
Private
Graduate Students: Yes
Setting: Urban

Stony Brook University, or the State University of New York at Stony Brook (PWI)
Stony Brook, NY
18,000 Undergraduates
Public
Graduate Students: Yes
Setting: Suburban

Walker, founder and CEO of Walker and Company Brands, which includes Bevel Shaving and Form Beauty, who majored in economics at the State University of New York–Stony Brook. These are two stellar examples of Black people who are using their liberal arts degree to the maximum. I love them for this, for real, but I still believe that when we don't steer our children toward a wealth-building major in college, we are subjecting them to professional chance.

What Can You Do with a Liberal Arts Degree?

For anyone who's offended by what I've said, I want to be clear that there is not only one way to succeed. Success after graduation is determined by hustle and by your child identifying what they're good at and maximizing their potential. Many of my Black college friends have liberal arts degrees—most of them I went to Wesleyan with—and several of them are successful and happy. My point about leading your children toward specific majors is a product of the world being different now from what it was twenty to thirty years ago. While "jobs" are changing and may become obsolete in their traditional form, business and technology are booming, with companies like Apple, Google, and IBM no longer requiring college degrees for positions in their company. Many of us were in college during the tech boom of the mid-nineties and had little idea of the explosion that was about to happen. Imagine if AfroTech had not gotten such a late start? What if we could have closed the digital divide earlier? I want my children—and yours—to be on the cutting edge of innovation, and that may mean being a liberal arts major (rare) or a student who is attuned to where the world is moving.

While my feelings about this are strong, many of my education professional peers, Black and white, do not see it the same way. They are adamant that students should seek colleges that "match" or "fit" their unique profile and not be so set on one academic direction. One Black high school counselor we interviewed wished that more Black parents did not suggest engineering and business

to their children. She implied that suggesting these majors and en-
suing careers stifles children's creativity and does not allow them to
create a career that may be better and maybe even more lucrative.

> *"If there was one thing I would tell Black parents, [it's] that there
> are more than five majors. When talking with many families,
> the only majors they think exist are premed, engineering, law,
> business, and education. There are so many more majors and
> jobs than in those five areas. If I could get them to understand
> that, their college list would be a lot more realistic."* (High school
> college counselor)

Her point is well taken. While some cultural groups historically
have pushed their children toward certain majors, that's not what
most Black people do, and I do not want to encourage a narrow view
of acceptable majors. Part of how we have survived as a people is by
being creative, innovative, and resourceful. Liberal arts education
builds these capacities, and I would never want to be dismissive of it.

Here are some careers derived from liberal arts degrees according to *U.S. News and World Report*:

- Advertising representative
- Archivist
- Artist
- Events director
- Financial analyst
- Graphic designer
- Human resources specialist
- Journalist
- Marketing specialist
- Public relations specialist
- Project manager
- Research analyst
- Social worker
- Statistician
- Teacher
- Technical writer
- Web developer

So What Is a Parent's Role in This?

Black parents should assess who their children are and who they're
becoming. We must educate ourselves and our children so that

everyone understands the choices they have. A liberal arts education may be exactly what your child needs at this stage of their life. It may give them the chance to explore a range of academic disciplines they were not exposed to in high school and so tap into a curiosity that leads not just to a career but to genuine intellectual satisfaction and personal happiness. I applaud parents who love, accept, and support their children in this way and have more faith than fear. Some parents see a job and money as the necessary outcome of a college education. My advice is to partner with your child and have a joint vision for their educational and professional lives. We do not have to force them into anything, but we have to help them see how certain majors can lead to certain career opportunities. I think we should encourage them to take economics or finance or investing courses. To take a computer coding class maybe or to stick with a foreign language. What I do not like to hear is when parents say, "It's their life. They need to figure it out." No. This leads to students graduating college after more years than anticipated and oftentimes with more debt accumulated. While we know that each child is different and that some children will thrive in an environment where they can choose courses that stimulate their mind and lead them to become fascinating people, I urge you to make sure that there is a plan and a safety net. If your child does not know why they're in college, maybe they shouldn't be there, or they need an adult to steer them in a direction that builds on strengths they may not recognize. I am not saying that business, engineering, computer science, and premed are the only options, but I am saying to be wary of majors that do not have a direct correlation with employment and wealth-building.

I am aware that there are data to refute my assertions. Much of what I'm saying is anecdotal and may be emotionally tied to my being an educator and seeing too many of the Black students I have worked with graduate with a liberal arts degree and then feel "stuck" professionally. They do not regret their college experience; what they question is whether they made the right choice for their financial future when they selected a major.

In late 2021, I posed a question on my Facebook page: "For those who went to college or those who intend to send their children to college, do you find a liberal arts degree to be useful? Why or why not?" Responses were one-sided, and most people, regardless of race, defended their opinion that a liberal arts education is extremely valuable. The comment that challenged my thinking the most was this: "I think it's often unfairly painted as being impractical—I think it's actually highly practical and skills-oriented, especially in a largely information and knowledge-based economy." I think this was accurate and more than fair. Another person likened a liberal arts major to a "utility player" in baseball, which implies versatility. I could also call a liberal arts major a "jack of all trades and a master of none." Another comment was "It's part of an educational foundation, necessary to compete in many chosen professions. It's a path you can use to go to professional school." That last part supports a point of mine: earning a liberal arts education often requires that you go on to graduate school to level up. For many Black families, that move will bring more debt. Another comment that deserves to be quoted came from a friend: "The cost of college vs the debt ratio is alarming. The average number of students who complete within four years is less than 53%. The debt is debilitating for some. Most of the students I work with cannot afford to do it." Money and college have a complicated relationship, and we will discuss it in chapter 10, "Show Me the Money."

I will always stand by the notion that cost, location, major, and career should be the core concerns when a family researches, applies to, and selects a college. I did not intend to convey the message that the liberal arts are bad or a one-way ticket to poverty. My hope is that this discussion of liberal arts as a luxury and preprofessional programs as a safer bet stirs your thinking about what's important for your family, the next educational steps for your child, and eventually both of your legacies. The next steps may not be immediately obvious, but now you have food for thought.

What's Best for Your Child?

HBCUs versus PWIs

Overview

Throughout our children's educational experience we, as Black parents, must think about the spaces in which we place our children. College is no different. Currently, there is a divide among many Black families and college counselors about which is better: PWIs or HBCUs. While both have their own merits, there are a lot of misconceptions about which institution type will best prepare students for success. It is imperative that we parents help our children recognize their gifts and explore which kind of school may be best for their total development.

Some Black children need an HBCU for support, identity development, and personal comfort; others may thrive in any environment or may be more comfortable at a PWI because that is what they are accustomed to or because it has the type of diversity they seek. *HBCUs should at least be a consideration for your student given HBCUs' long track record of success across all disciplines.* However, if your vision for your child or, more importantly, their vision for themselves is of a PWI, make sure you have clear reasons for the choice and a plan for how to achieve success there.

––––––––

At every stage of raising a child, we parents ask ourselves, "What will be best for my child?" In many of our life decisions, we do what we believe will give our children opportunities that we did not have or what we think would have benefited our own childhoods. We do our best to keep our children safe, healthy, and well educated. When it comes to their schooling, and according to our financial resources, we spend a lot of time considering their educational options: we evaluate the school district we reside in; we may weigh the pros and cons of private versus public education and estimate how much we are willing to pay for primary and secondary education; and we contemplate the many trade-offs we could make to help mold our children into who they will become. How will the school they attend affect their identity, development, and friend group? Will I as a parent have to worry about racism or other forms of discrimination? In a 2019 story in the *Washington Post* titled "The Tough Choices Black Parents Face When Choosing a School for Their Children," many parents interviewed for the story described the tough decisions they faced when examining educational choices. One parent called it the "head versus heart" dilemma. When a school that's a better option academically lacks racial diversity, there is almost always a price a Black child will pay in terms of their sense of self. As a parent, your head tells you that putting them in a high-ranking public school or private school is a smart decision. But your heart aches at the thought of what your child may have to endure there. There are so many factors that we as Black parents must consider to ensure that our children have the best chance at success and an equal opportunity. Just like many of our thoughts and actions as parents are informed by our personal experiences growing up, both good and bad, so are our perceptions of college.

When I (Tim) think back to the many things that drew me to my college of choice, I would say there was really no choice to be made. The choice was cemented in the brotherhood of Morehouse College, in the thriving Black affluence of the city of Atlanta, and with the deep indoctrination in Black culture that came with attending an HBCU. When I think back on those years at Morehouse, yes, my academic experience was rich and helped shape the person I became, but it was the environment, support, and the constant affirmation of who I was as a Black man that framed those years the most. I came from a predominantly white high school and community in Arlington, Texas, and I found at Morehouse more than a college education; Morehouse helped me better understand my identity as a young Black man in America. The school gave me the confidence to go out into the world and instilled in me the necessity to serve. I understood my value and would not be discouraged by the many challenges of being Black in America.

My wife had a much different upbringing in Country Club Hills, a south suburb of Chicago. Both her older brother and sister went to college and her father completed his doctorate, but there was no one outside her immediate family who attended college. As the youngest in the family who got some guidance from her siblings, she maintains that she was very misinformed about the process of the college search. She excelled in Advanced Placement courses, was involved in activities, and scored well on the ACT; however, with poor guidance, she applied to only two schools: Hampton University and the University of Miami. She chose to swap the harsh winters of Chicago for mild winters on the beaches of South Florida.

University of Miami (PWI)
Coral Gables, FL
11,000 Undergraduates
Private
Graduate Students: Yes
Setting: Urban

As she and I got to know each other as friends, one thing became evident: our college days were stark contrasts. Where I would talk about being on the yard and hanging out in Atlanta, she would tell me about watching games in the Miami Orange Bowl in the rain with more than sixty thousand fans, hanging out on South Beach, and wearing flip-flops all year long. And while my experience was defined by "traditional" Black culture and experiences, she was experiencing her Blackness in an entirely different way. Having graduated from a largely Black and Latinx high school, she found her transition to the University of Miami to be a bit of a shock. The campus exposed her to how variant being Black could be. She had her first experience being identified as an American Black among

Bahamians, Jamaicans, and Haitians, together with affluent white, Cuban, and international classmates. My college experience largely strengthened my identity, yet she learned how to cling to hers differently. Naïvely drawn to the school because of the academics, beautiful campus, and strong sports reputation of "The U," she received a quick lesson in socioeconomics and experienced being an "only" in the classroom. While her time at Miami was rich in culture, there were moments defined by self-segregation, as described in the modern classic *Why Are All the Black Kids Sitting Together in the Cafeteria?* by Dr. Beverly Daniel Tatum, who is a Wesleyan University graduate and former Spelman College president.

During our time dating and in the early years of our marriage, we enjoyed talking about our different college experiences, along with the pros and cons that came with attending a PWI versus an HBCU. Our conversations were never about which one was better; rather, we talked about the experiences, socialization, and preparation for life that each type provided. We both considered ourselves successful in our professions, and neither of us questioned whether anything would have been better for us had we attended another college. It was not until we had children that the question arose. My wife dressed the children in Hurricanes clothes for Saturday games, while giving my mom the side-eye for putting them in University of Michigan gear, where she had attended as an undergraduate student in the 1960s. At the same time, I would talk about the day my son would attend Morehouse. Once they were toddlers, we had to think about where they may want to go to college and to imagine how those conversations would go. Like most parents who want their children to go to college, we would like our children to make informed decisions and do what is best for themselves.

University of Michigan (PWI)
Ann Arbor, MI
31,000 Undergraduates
Public
Graduate Students: Yes
Setting: Midsize City

In the introduction we said there are three camps of Black families on the question of HBCUs versus PWIs:

1. Those that believe PWIs are inherently better than HBCUs because they will offer their child a better chance at monetary success in life; these families will not consider HBCUs.
2. Those with parents who attended an HBCU and want their child to follow in their footsteps; these parents dismiss the idea of their child attending a PWI.
3. Those that will consider *all* institutions and let the decision be guided by financial aid or scholarships received, location, majors offered, and ultimately what's best for their family situation.

Vanderbilt University (PWI)
Nashville, TN
13,000 Undergraduates
Private
Graduate Students: Yes
Setting: Urban

While the third camp is probably the largest, the first two make the most noise. Their preference usually drives the college search process. All three camps are justified in their thinking based on their lived experience; we do think it's very important, though, to enter the college search process with a mind open to both institutional types and to be guided by the needs of your child.

American University (PWI)
Washington, DC
8,000 Undergraduates
Private
Graduate Students: Yes
Setting: Urban

George Washington University (PWI)
Washington, DC
12,000 Undergraduates
Private
Graduate Students: Yes
Setting: Urban

One of the best ways to identify which type is a better fit is simply to expose your child to both types of institution. Later in the book we will talk in depth about the college visit. To get a sense of what a school can offer, you can do no better than to walk around the campus, look at the buildings, talk to students and staff, and learn about the history of the school. Families living in the South and Mid-Atlantic have plenty of HBCUs within driving distance to visit. Families living in other parts of the

University of Maryland (PWI)
College Park, MD
30,000 Undergraduates
Public
Graduate Students: Yes
Setting: Suburban

Georgetown University (PWI)
Washington, DC
5,500 Undergraduates
Private
Graduate Students: Yes
Setting: Urban

country—the Midwest and the Mountain and Pacific time zones—live far from most HBCUs. But with proper planning, you can visit multiple campuses on a trip. For example, if you go to Nashville to visit Vanderbilt, be sure to visit Fisk and Tennessee State; if you go to Washington, DC, to see Howard, make stops also at American University, George Washington University, the University of Maryland, or Georgetown; you could then travel the short way to Baltimore to visit Johns Hopkins, Bowie State, and Morgan State; if you are in Atlanta looking at Georgia Tech or Emory, you could also look at Clark Atlanta, Morehouse, or Spelman; and if you go to New Orleans to tour Tulane, you can also visit Xavier and Dillard. In many major cities in the Central or Eastern time zone, you can tour both types of institution.

As you begin to think about the college search process, you must begin to evaluate as a family what is best for the student, with careful consideration of cost, location, major, and career. Moreover, given the current climate in the United States, we also encourage families to factor in how a school defines diversity, the resources and support it gives to Black students, and the cultural climate on its campus. We find that many parents and college counselors put a lot of emphasis on cost, location, major, and career and pay less attention to the social experiences outside formal education. Given all these factors, we think that Black families should consider both HBCUs and PWIs as viable options in their college search.

Understanding your child's level of self-

Bowie State University (HBCU)
Bowie, MD
5,400 Undergraduates
Public
Graduate Students: Yes
Setting: Suburban

Georgia Institute of Technology (PWI)
Atlanta, GA
16,500 Undergraduates
Public
Graduate Students: Yes
Setting: Urban

Emory University (PWI)
Atlanta, GA
7,000 Undergraduates
Private
Graduate Students: Yes
Setting: Suburban

Clark Atlanta University (HBCU)
Atlanta, GA
3,100 Undergraduates
Private
Graduate Students: Yes
Setting: Urban

Tulane University (PWI)
New Orleans, LA
7,700 Undergraduates
Private
Graduate Students: Yes
Setting: Urban

awareness about their Black cultural identity should partially inform where you suggest they attend college. College should be a place where they will make progress as a young Black adult among other ambitious young Black adults. Historically, this has occurred at HBCUs and at prestigious PWIs such as Duke, the University of Virginia, Stanford, Northwestern, Georgetown, Emory, Wesleyan, and Amherst College. These schools have excellent reputations for having substantial, supportive Black populations with which students can engage during the college years and network after graduation. While none of the PWIs have the same level of intense HBCU familial love, if your child is a strong student, these schools need to be part of your exploration, according to your child's strengths and interests. There are many notable colleges and universities with great academic programs, facilities, and reputations of excellence, but we parents must ask ourselves a question: Do the schools have what my child needs to succeed both inside and outside the classroom?

In addition to cultural identity and the fit of a college campus, it's paramount that your student considers places where they feel they will be academically productive, be socially engaged, and have access to the tools they need to make moves toward a career. Throughout the college search process they must assess their strengths, weaknesses, and interests and determine what major or areas

Dillard University (HBCU)
New Orleans, LA
1,100 Undergraduates
Private
Graduate Students: Yes
Setting: Urban

Duke University (PWI)
Durham, NC
6,500 Undergraduates
Private
Graduate Students: Yes
Setting: Suburban

University of Virginia (PWI)
Charlottesville, VA
18,066 Undergraduates
Public
Graduate Students: Yes
Setting: Midsize City

Stanford University (PWI)
Palo Alto, CA
6,500 Undergraduates
Private
Graduate Students: Yes
Setting: Suburban

Northwestern University (PWI)
Evanston, IL
8,400 Undergraduates
Private
Graduate Students: Yes
Setting: Urban

Amherst College (PWI)
Amherst, MA
1,800 Undergraduates
Private
Graduate Students: No
Setting: Remote

of study make the most sense for them in the short and long terms. There are any number of things that can help students fit in at a school such as connections with faculty, student organizations they identify with, support staff that help them navigate college life, and a campus that makes them feel they truly belong. The reality is that their interests will probably evolve, just as we parents continue to learn more about ourselves, but what is important is that they find schools that will give them options and won't limit their development in any way. College should not only be a place where students gain a formal education; it's also just as important, we would argue, that the college experience prepare them for self-leadership in their adult lives. Acclaimed author Malcolm Gladwell, in an interview on the College Guidance Network, advised students in the search for colleges to ask themselves the following questions:

1. What do I want my college experience to be like?
2. What do I care about?
3. What motivates me?
4. What do I stand for?

These are questions that need serious reflection.

Now, when we talk about HBCUs and PWIs, we must deal with the elephant in the room: *resources.* If there is one universal frustration expressed by parents and students about HBCUs compared with many elite PWIs, it's the physical plant. HBCUs' campus facilities (dorms, labs, gyms, etc.) and on-campus dining options are sometimes not to families' liking. Couple that with the surrounding area of some HBCUs—southwest Atlanta, for instance, or Washington, DC. Some Black families fear their child is not "built" to navigate an environment with an element of the "hood." There have been several instances in helping and working with families that they have admitted that their child is unprepared for an HBCU environment without pristine landscaping or with an understandably jealous local population that likes to prey on young and naïve students. A similar worry, however, may keep these same students from enrolling on a rural PWI campus when they have lived their lives in suburban or urban neighborhoods and want to avoid being subjected to blatant racism.

In the interviews and roundtables we had with families, HBCU and PWI graduates, and college counselors, we asked why some Black families were resistant to considering HBCUs. In reply, all the groups had the perception that HBCUs are physically not as well equipped as their PWI counterparts. Some institutions like Harvard, Princeton, Yale, and Stanford have very large endowments that no HBCU could compete with, but resources extend beyond endowments. It's important also to think about what resources your individual student needs. Is it access to faculty and staff for academic support? Is it residential halls with programming for their academic interest? Intramural sports? Study abroad? Scholarships and financial aid? No matter what institutional type, a school may have all the resources most students want yet lack a certain resource your student discovers they desire. If you don't establish as a family what resources you need, you are doing a disservice to your student as you go through the college search process.

The title of this chapter may be a bit misleading. We are not making an argument for either HBCUs or PWIs. There is no one clear answer for what type of school is better for all Black children. But we do implore Black families to have a firm understanding of the choices. We hope that you will repeatedly evaluate cost (debt), location, major, and career, while also giving priority to identity and campus amenities. Over all of these considerations is the umbrella of cultural experience that, as proud Black people, we cannot ignore, and we must help our children be proud of who they are in an environment that accepts them.

Above all, safety must be a priority: physical and emotional. There is no guarantee that any one environment will be better than another, but you must take your child's temperature about where they will be most comfortable and confident that they can succeed. Yes, there is the consideration that true growth happens in discomfort, but there is a time and a place for that. For students who are seventeen or eighteen years old, there are advantages to not placing them in a drastically unfamiliar environment to prove a point about their needing to be among Black people at an HBCU or needing to be forced into the "real world" of a PWI. Safety first.

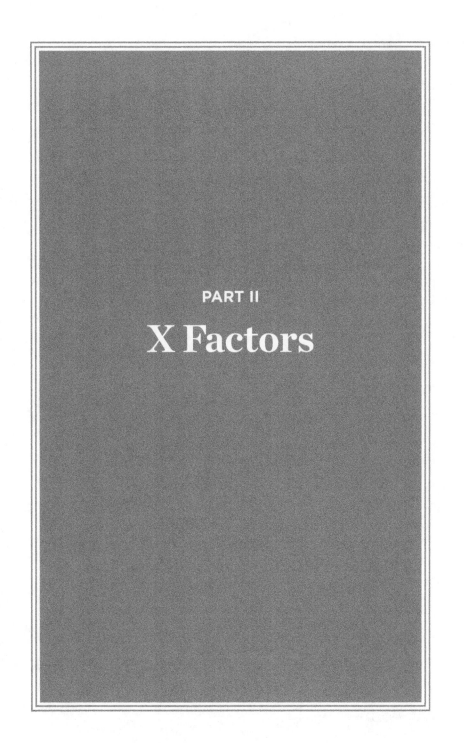

PART II

X Factors

CHAPTER 6

What Questions Should You Be Asking in Your Family?

Overview

As your family begins to think about the educational choices facing your student, it's important to consider how those decisions will affect the college admissions process years down the line. Long before a student applies to college or even attends high school, many questions need to be considered:

1. How will you pay for your student's education?
2. Will your student attend public or private schools?
3. What courses will they need to take in preparation for college?

More than anything, your family needs to have clear and active communication together. You must know what questions each person involved should be asking as you plan for all aspects of the college admissions process—from academic, financial, and cultural perspectives.

Managing the partnership between parent and child during the admissions process is incredibly challenging. Like all partnerships, whether it be in a business, the game of spades, or a marriage, ideally it is a fifty-fifty relationship. We all know, however, that an even split is far from the reality in most instances. No matter what the nature of the relationship, communication is critical to reducing tension and misunderstanding. Communication will be paramount as your family begins the college admissions process and ultimately decides on a school that is beneficial for both child and family.

When it comes to parenthood, partnership takes on many forms. We would like to think that no matter the condition of the parents' relationship, their child's health and well-being, and a wish for the child's success in life, is something the parents can agree on. We believe that the ideal is to have two caring and responsible parents in a household, but we also know that this isn't everyone's reality or wish. Regardless of the makeup of the household, the educational choices made for a child from infancy through college can be difficult to make and, in many instances, require constant input from parents and caregivers. In a survey of Black parents, when asked if they agreed with their partner on educational philosophies, only 50 percent said yes and 28 percent said "for the most part." No matter whether you are part of a happily married couple or a single parent managing child-rearing alone, the conversation around educational choices for children is a complicated one.

Every family situation is unique, and it would be unrealistic for us to think that we can answer all of the questions that families will have about the college search. Still, we think it's important to address some of the fundamental ones. In appendix B, "Frequently Asked Questions," we provide many questions and answers that you can discuss as a family as you conduct your college search. Below, we provide some context for the questions to facilitate what can sometimes be challenging conversations.

Public versus Private

In our survey of Black parents, we found that, in many instances, their own K–12 educational experiences had a great deal of influence on how they wanted their children educated. In most cases, if both parents went to public school, they believed that public school would be adequate for their children, and those who went to private or independent school felt strongly that their children should have a similar educational experience. This holds true for Shereem and me (Tim) too. Shereem went to private school and has sent his children to private school as well. I (Tim) went to public school and am a strong advocate of public school. What happens, however, when parents had different educational experiences? Now, we understand that for a lot of families, not just Black families, sending a child to an independent, boarding, or private school is not a viable option given the cost. We also understand that, depending on where you live, there may be few good public options, which further complicates this conversation and relates to a bigger conversation about equity of access to education. For those of us, however, who do have viable public and private options, the question of whether public or private school is the better option is a valid one to ask. There are pros and cons to both that you should take into consideration.

Here are some questions to think about:

1. Why is your family considering private school?
2. Does your student have particular needs?
3. Are there few good public options in your area?
4. Is there a particular curriculum offered by a private school that you think your child can benefit from?
5. Do you believe that private school can offer the best overall educational preparation for your child?
6. Is your family prepared to invest in private school in the formative years in addition to paying the cost of post-secondary education?

If you are thinking that going to a private school will automatically give your student a leg up in getting into a top college, that is simply not true. We address this topic in more depth in chapter 7, "Perception versus Reality."

The debate over private and public school often comes down to cost. In choosing to have your child attend public school, you may not be paying the school directly, but there are indirect costs if you are paying for a home or renting in a public school district in an affluent area. Thus, if you are considering public schooling for your child, the question of where you plan to live must be at the center of family conversations early on. Bear in mind that, compared with private schools, many public schools have larger class sizes, fewer individualized resources for students, and a more standardized curriculum, which can be limiting to some students. While most public schools do not have the small class sizes and rich resources of private schools, they often are more racially and socioeconomically diverse. If diversity is something that you and your family value, then that is a factor you'll want to weigh when considering educational options.

Is College the Best Option?

When many of us parents were growing up, we had three options after high school: go to college, join the military, or get a job. With the advent of the internet, social media, and online selling platforms like eBay and Etsy, there are new avenues open to making money and creating a business that were not available ten or fifteen years ago. Plus, many companies, such as Google and Apple, no longer require that applicants have a college degree to get hired. Given these new opportunities, many of them in entrepreneurship, parents may ask why their child has to go to college at all. While the data still point to postsecondary education creating higher levels of lifelong earnings, it's clear that there has been a significant shift in the labor marketplace and the preparation needed for entry. So, families should discuss whether college is the right plan for your student. Clearly things can change, but leading up to and through high school, everyone should be on the same page about whether going to college is a priority. The educational decisions made in preparation for college—in course selection, savings options, and extracurricular activities—are far different from decisions made when college is not the goal. In either case, everyone must agree on the plan before a student proceeds through high school because once the student enters high school, it can be hard to change their trajectory.

Our advice would always be to prepare in middle school and high school as though your child will go to college because, if there is a change in plan, it is much easier to shift when your student has a strong academic foundation than when they don't. It is during the formative years that students often develop their interests and passions. We believe that families should support these interests, but we don't think that support should come at the expense of the student's academic preparation, which can also help to nurture those interests. Regardless of the student's trajectory, it's important to discuss what the long-term goals are. Some students are just not meant to go to college, and that's fine. There are students who are destined to be soldiers, and there are those whose entrepreneurial spirit will drive their life choices. There is no right or wrong way to go, but it's important that parents and guardians have a plan in place.

Funding College

If there is agreement that the goal is college, then the conversation about how the student's college education will be paid for must happen early on. College is expensive, and the cost of college is not going down anytime soon.

I (Tim) have often said getting into college is easy; paying for college is the hard part. Yes, there are a lot of schools that offer great financial aid to support families, but the truth is that the more money and assets you have as a family, the less need-based aid you are likely to be offered by financial aid offices. Given how aid is calculated, many middle- and upper-class families have difficulty securing the financial aid they believe they deserve. This can be frustrating to families who fall into this category; thus the parents in these families should talk to their child about how they are going to pay for and save for college sooner rather than later. These conversations may influence the decision of where the child can apply.

Additionally, with the evolution of affirmative action and how it's regulated, the idea of a "minority" scholarship is not as pervasive as it was thirty years ago. So, if you are counting on scholarship money to help fund your child's college experience, that is a possibility you'll want to explore prior to their senior year. In chapter 10, "Show Me the Money," we discuss financial aid in some detail.

How Far Away Is Too Far?

Families must ask early on, How far away is too far? Are there any geographical limits to the schools your student will apply to? With social media, email, and teleconferencing technology made popular in the pandemic, it's easy to stay connected at a distance, but there are other factors to consider related to a school's location. Public colleges and universities located outside your family's state of residence will charge higher tuition to out-of-state students. There is also the expense of plane or train tickets if students decide to go to a school far from home. Finally, there is the consideration for parents of how long it will take to reach their child should something happen. Families may be open to negotiating the matter of distance, but the matter should be addressed early in the college search process to manage expectations for everyone.

In addition to distance, there is also the question of *where* parents are willing to let their children go to school. When we spoke with parents in preparing to write this book, several parents were adamant about states and regions where they would not want their students to attend school. One family said, "We know our daughter is looking to play Division I volleyball in college, but there are certain schools that we know we are not even going to consider because we worry about our daughter being in certain states." While much of this hesitancy and concern is driven by the current social climate in the country, it is also driven by regional bias, stereotypes, and personal experiences. One parent explained, "I know I would not want my student to apply to [school X] because when I visited there when I was applying to college in the eighties, I was called the N-word and would not want my child considering it even if it is now considered one of the top schools in the country."

Although this event happened nearly forty years ago, such events can stick in a parent's memory and influence where they feel comfortable sending their children to school. Many would argue that a lot has changed in our country since the eighties and nineties, but the counterargument can be made that little has changed. If there are locations that parents have concerns with, it is important that they explain to their child where the concerns come from. Finally, we would encourage parents to reach out to schools they have concerns with and ask those schools how they are supporting Black students and ensuring their academic success, safety, and cultural support.

Return on Investment

We started this chapter talking about partnerships. For any partnership you have, you want it to be a success, and how success is defined varies. Everyone is looking for return on investment, or ROI, and the college experience is no different. When families begin to think about college, they must determine what college success looks like.

1. Is success graduating and being debt free?
2. Is it finishing in four years with a job in hand?
3. Is it being able to say you attended one of the top institutions in the country?
4. Is there some other standard that will define success for your student in the college experience?

The reality is that apart from attending a school for brand recognition, the other criteria of success can be met at many institutions in the country.

It is easier, of course, to access certain resources and opportunities at some institutions than at others. If a student decides to attend Emory and is interested in premed, do they have an advantage over a student at Agnes Scott College or Georgia State University when it comes to access to hospitals and clinics? Maybe, due to proximity. But does having access to those resources guarantee a greater chance of admission to medical school than students have at the other schools? **No.** We hope that you will take away many messages from this book, but one of them is that name and or brand recognition will only go so far. Many people think that if their child goes to school X, then things will be easier upon graduation, but the reality is that schools at all levels are looking for the best students, not average students who happened to attend good schools. Only you and your family can define what success is in the college experience. If there is an experience your family is looking for from college, begin discussing it early.

Agnes Scott College (PWI)
Decatur, GA
1,000 Undergraduates
Private
Graduate Students: No
Setting: Suburban

Georgia State University (PWI)
Atlanta, GA
22,000 Undergraduates
Private
Graduate Students: Yes
Setting: Urban

What's Driving the Decision-Making?

In *The Truth about College Admission*, authors Brennan Barnard and Rick Clark describe four critical areas, or wedges as they call them, that often trip families up as they navigate the college search process: time, communication, money, and ego. We have addressed the importance of starting early, having clear communication, and discussing money, and we also want to discuss what may be the biggest obstacle in the process: the presence of ego. Barnard and Clark are forthright about how families should approach the admissions experience: "For the sake of family relationships, parents and students must put their egos in the box." When it comes to the ego of Black parents, we know that some parents are determined that the money they spend on their child's higher education is going to the HBCU from which they graduated, whereas others think that HBCUs are inferior schools and so don't consider them at all for their child. What should be driving the process of selecting a school, however, is what is best for the student's development.

Should parents have a say in the college search process? Of course. We advocate for that throughout the book, but it is the student, after all, who will have to live with the decision that gets made. We would hope that there is room for the student to articulate what they are looking for and to explore the many college options available to them. It's important that the student have a voice that is listened to and respected. In other words, everyone involved needs to keep an open mind.

There is a joke in college admissions that the answer to any question is "it depends." How much financial aid will I receive? It depends. What are my chances of getting in? It depends. Can I graduate in four years? It depends. Will I have a job or acceptance to a graduate school upon graduation? It depends. The college search process can be confusing and complicated without proper direction. That is why there is a booming industry of independent college counseling professionals—like Shereem's company Strategic Admissions Advice—that help families navigate the college search process. Many of these admissions consultants are great at what they do because of their understanding of the process and access to information, but their greatest strength is in providing direction to families, and that begins with knowing what colleges are looking for and what questions to ask a family to find the right fit.

CHAPTER 7

Perception versus Reality

Overview

College admissions is a mysterious process, and each school has its own set of standards for decision-making. As families begin the college search process, there are a lot of assumptions they may make from not understanding the context and nuances of admissions or from having wrong information picked up from the "wine and cheese circuit," as we like to call it. We have spent a lot of time answering families' questions about the mysteries of college admissions, and we have certainly spent time dispelling myths and correcting misinformation that spreads through neighborhoods and schools. In this chapter we explore some of the most common misperceptions that add to the anxiety already built into college admissions.

———

There are a lot of things that stand out in our almost fifty years of combined work in secondary and higher education. One of these is the disconnect between perception and reality surrounding the college admissions process. Oftentimes people have strong opinions about what it takes to get into top schools or what goes into preparing a strong application. Many of these opinions are held by parents who saw their child get into their first-choice school. Sometimes an admissions officer claims to have an insider track and offers advice that is not applicable to every institution. **In reality, there is no formula that guarantees admission at top colleges and universities.** Most admissions decisions are influenced by an individual school's needs, or what we in the profession call "institutional priorities." These priorities can vary from year to year and may take into account athletic programs, development (institutional advancement or donations), geography, academic interest, the need for members in the marching band or on the debate team, the desire for a student from a specific state, or any number of other priorities that institutions consider in composing their incoming class.

PWIs Are Better Than HBCUs

One of the most surprising things we found from one of our surveys of Black parents was that 92 percent of them believe that there is a perception that PWIs are "better" than HBCUs.

> "As I was going through my college admission process, it was made clear to me by my college counseling office that in order for me to be successful, I should attend a PWI. Morehouse was viewed as a safety school." (Graduate of the University of Virginia)

> "Our daughter knew she wanted to go to a competitive school like University of Pennsylvania or another of the Ivies; she ultimately ended up at Columbia through Early Decision. But as she was going through the process, Spelman was never an option, despite my efforts, and a lot of that had to do with the culture of her independent school. The fact that not many students considered HBCUs mainly because there is a lack of HBCU exposure in California." (Alumni of Spelman and Williams College)

University of Pennsylvania (PWI)
Philadelphia, PA
10,000 Undergraduates
Private
Graduate Students: Yes
Setting: Urban

Williams College (PWI)
Williamstown, MA
2,000 Undergraduates
Private
Graduate Students: No
Setting: Remote

We understand the many reasons for this survey finding, yet there is a fundamental question here about what makes up "better." Is better having more resources? A larger endowment? Is better being diverse? Or is better simply a matter of name recognition or ranking by *U.S. News and World Report*? Many don't know that those rankings are calculated with variables that are not directly related to students' undergraduate experience on campus. Some of the variables include the school's selectivity based on test scores and class rank, the rate of alumni giving, and the academic reputation of the school, but ethnic and racial diversity are currently not calculated in the rankings. There may be solid arguments for why the ranking variables are what they are, but it can also be argued that they do not speak directly to student experiences, the support services offered, or the campus climate that students will experience daily. Thus, if you emphasize rank when selecting schools, it's important that you understand what those rankings mean for your child.

To answer the question of whether HBCUs or PWIs are better, you must define what *better* means to you. So often, *better* is defined by someone outside your home or by circumstances or variables that don't speak directly to your child's needs. There can be so many things that go into determining whether something is better, and the reality is that it's subjective. Most college graduates, no matter what type of school they went to, think their school is better than others for any number of reasons. As we enter the college search process with our children, however, we can't depend solely on what we think we know. It's important that we keep an open mind, do the research, visit the campuses, and think beyond ourselves and own circles.

Black Lives Matter

Yes, Black lives matter in college admissions, but the reality is that all lives matter in college admissions, especially at the most prestigious schools. Affirmative action policies that existed in the 1970s, 1980s, and 1990s are no longer enacted in the same way in college admissions. Several lawsuits challenging affirmative action policies have reached the Supreme Court. Given the battle over considering race in college admissions, the notion of "minority" or "Black" scholarships or of Black applicants having a leg up is often untrue. For students looking to apply to the top schools in the country, the bar to clear starts with having great grades, continues with an applicant separating themselves from their peers, and then goes on to what the applicant can add to the campus. Are schools completely blind to race in admissions? No, but neither are they making decisions based on that one aspect of an applicant.

One thing to know when you come across the word *diversity* in higher education is that its meaning is inclusive and comprehensive. When many of the parents who are reading this book went to college, schools recruited Black, Hispanic, and Native students directly; today, schools use much more inclusive terms like *underrepresented*, *students of color*, or *BIPOC*. These terms are more inclusive, yes, but they also lump groups together as though they were all the same. Thus, when having conversations about diversity on college campuses, it's important to be intentional in the language you use. If you ask about Black students, they may be grouped under these umbrella terms, which may not yield the answers you are looking for. In many instances *diversity* refers to geographic origin, citizenship, socioeconomic status,

The Supreme Court on Affirmative Action in Higher Education

1978: In *Regents of the University of California v. Bakke,* the court ruled that the medical school at the University of California, Davis, could not reserve some slots with separate admissions standards for minority applicants. But the court also ruled that colleges could consider race and ethnicity in admissions decisions in ways that did not create quotas.

2003: In *Gratz v. Bollinger,* the court ruled that the University of Michigan at Ann Arbor had unconstitutionally used an undergraduate admissions system in which underrepresented minority applicants received points for their ethnicity or race.

2003: In *Grutter v. Bollinger,* the court ruled that the University of Michigan's law school was within its constitutional rights in considering applicants' race or ethnicity because it did so through a "holistic" review and not by simply awarding points for race or ethnicity.

2013: In *Fisher v. University of Texas at Austin,* the court ruled that lower courts needed to apply "strict scrutiny" and not give colleges deference when reviewing legal challenges to colleges' consideration of race and ethnicity in admissions decisions.

Source: https://www.insidehighered.com /news/2016/06/24/supreme-court -upholds-consideration-race-admissions being first generation, and other factors. *Diversity*, especially at PWIs, has become this catch-all term to keep in step with the growing diversity, equity, and inclusion initiatives in our country, but how schools define *diversity* may change based on the audience. Both PWIs and HBCUs are looking to expand the diversity on their campuses, given the changing demographics of our country and heightened awareness of a need for greater access and social justice.

BIPOC stands for Black, Indigenous, People of Color

Going to a "Good" High School Helps

Can going to a competitive high school help you in your college preparation? Yes. Does going to a high school (public or private) with a good reputation ensure you will get into the college of your choice? No. Not everyone has a good public school in their neighborhood to attend, with a curriculum and resources to support the multiple needs of its students. With any school that you send your student to, your student must take advantage of the opportunities and the resources available. So often I (Tim) review applications from students from private schools, where the students got good grades but did not take advantage of the academic and extracurricular opportunities offered at the schools given all of their resources. When I see this I am frustrated because many of these students have had plentiful opportunities, but they did not challenge themselves like their peers did. There is a belief in some Black families that if they just send their child to a "good" high school and the child does well, the name of the school will open doors to colleges and universities that would not have opened had they attended a school of less renown. Yes, there are instances when this happens, but colleges and universities focus on what the student did while at that school in comparison with their peers. Going to a competitive school can put a student in a hyper-competitive environment for which they may not be prepared. When it comes to top colleges and universities, where a student attended high school really means relatively little when stacked against what they were able to do with what they encountered there.

Testing: Does It Matter?

In chapter 12, we will go into depth about standardized testing and how it fits into the admissions process, but here we provide a quick assessment of how testing is perceived. The truth is that it varies among colleges. COVID-19 made many more schools become *test-optional*, *test-blind*, or some other variation that gives students the option to submit scores. It will be interesting to see how institutions and testing agencies respond when things return to normal. Some schools may remain test-optional, joining the subset of schools that were test-optional prior to the pandemic. These schools can be found at Fair Test, fairtest.org. However, many colleges and universities in the country will likely go back to requiring tests in some fashion, rejoining those that never suspended the requirement.

Students can have a great test score, but no matter how great it is, it probably will not take precedent over the courses and grades on a student's transcript over the course of their high school career. The same is true on the other end of the spectrum. A student may have what is perceived to be a low test score; however, if they have taken rigorous courses and have good grades, that low test score might be overlooked. When you think about testing, it's best to remember that it's just a number; and for the most selective schools in the country, know that it takes more than just a single number, whether GPA or test score, to be admitted.

The Rumor Mill

We want to make sure that you are aware that all information is not good information. When it comes to college admissions, we have discovered that many people who have gone through the process one or two times feel equipped to share information about how the process works. What we like to call "admissions fake news" is something you will often hear on the "wine and cheese circuit." This happens when gossipy parents exaggerate stories when they don't know why their student was admitted. All parents want their children to be seen in the best light, and what they say happened in admissions is probably just a small part of the file that resulted in the applicant's admission. There are perceptions of what it takes to get into selective schools that are far from the reality. We want you to be informed about the realities that take place in admissions and not depend on misguided information given how subjective admissions can be.

As parents, you know your child best and know what is best for them. I always encourage parents and students to reach out to ask schools questions they want answered and to seek clarification on things that are not clear. Above all, put your child before the ranking or academic reputation of the school. There will come a time when your child arrives on campus, and they alone must deal with the realities of the college choice they have made and the environment they are in.

As you and your family explore colleges, we encourage you to use all the resources at your disposal. While we are happy you are reading this book, this is just one of many resources. We advise you to research each school you are looking at and be in communication with its admissions staff, who will give you the right information to help separate perception from reality.

Case Study

We conclude this chapter with a thought exercise that we invite you to complete. High school and college admissions offices often use *case studies* to put students and parents in the seat of the admissions officer, from where they get a glimpse at how decisions are made based on class needs and institutional priorities. Imagine that you are an admissions officer for a university and must determine the **one** student of four who will be admitted to the incoming class. Please review the profiles of the four students in the table on the next page and read the institutional statistics and priorities listed below before making your determination.

All four applicants are Black and applying to the university's College of Arts and Sciences. The university has asked its admissions officers to consider the following when reviewing applicants:

- The university is looking for outgoing students who will add to the university community.
- Average GPA of the students admitted last year: 3.4.
- The university is test-optional; however, 50 percent of last year's applicants opted to submit scores. The average scores of last year's admitted students were 1150 for the SAT and 24 for the ACT.

The university wants its admissions officers to make the following decisions about the four applicants:

- Admit (1)
- Waitlist (1)
- Deny (2)

Be assured that our case study is oversimplified. There are other factors used to evaluate applicants, of course—among them: essays, letters of recommendations, and the rigor of high school courses taken.

Case Study

Attribute	Student 1	Student 2	Student 3	Student 4
Gender	Male	Female	Female	Male
GPA	3.2	4.0	3.5	2.9
Test score	ACT 23	Did not submit	SAT 1000	ACT 33
High school	Independent	Public	Charter	Home-schooled
Activities	President of student government association, member of school band, involved in church	Worked 30 hours a week in high school, very little school involvement	Started robotics club, president of chemistry club, Girl Scout	Trained for an Olympic sport
Other information	Both parents are doctors	Single-parent household, parent did not attend college	Lives with mother, who went to college and is a corporate executive	Both parents have a college degree and own their own business

Decision:
admit (1)
waitlist (1)
deny (2)

CHAPTER 8

Gender Wars

How Black Males and Black Females
Are Assessed in College Admissions

Overview

There is a growing gender imbalance throughout US higher education at both PWIs and HBCUs. Among Black students applying to college, this imbalance is amplified, with significantly more Black females applying than males. This disparity creates challenges for college admissions offices trying to build a balanced incoming class. One challenge is how to increase the number of Black males applying to college; another challenge is avoiding the collateral damage that can happen when Black female applicants are not reviewed by the same standards as their male counterparts. This chapter looks at some of the dynamics that influence why Black males receive preference over Black females, especially at selective colleges and universities.

―――――――

Stephen A. Smith, a graduate of Winston-Salem State University in North Carolina and cohost of the popular show *First Take* on ESPN, often gives this response to an accusation that something was not fair: "Fair is a place where they judge pigs." While this sentiment could be applied to many parts of life, it could be no truer than in college admissions. Little about college admissions is fair, especially at selective colleges. As each year passes, application numbers continue to rise, with many application platforms allowing students to apply to multiple schools at one time; admit rates continue to go down as a direct result of the increase in applications; and college admissions decision-making becomes harder and harder for students, parents, and college counselors to understand. At many of the top schools in the country, there are far fewer spaces available than there are applicants, with admit rates being as low as 5 percent at schools such as Stanford and Harvard. That means that 95 percent of the students who applied to that school were denied admission. When asked about the competitive nature of admissions and the low admit rates, a dean at one of the nation's most selective institutions commented, "It's turning into a sweepstakes."

> For schools that your family is considering, look up the gender balance of the student body, if that is a consideration in your college search.

When schools build their incoming class, they should ideally consider factors beyond grades, test scores, activities, essays, and courses taken. They factor in class size; institutional priorities such as gender balance, legacy applicants, athletic recruits, artistic contributors, and academic interest; and university priorities for educational, socioeconomic, geographic, and racial diversity. On top of all of this, schools must balance a financial aid budget. The more competitive a school is, the less fair the outcome is for most applicants.

When co-ed institutions form their first-year class, the goal for most is to get as close to a fifty-fifty gender balance as possible to achieve gender parity in the classroom and some semblance of fairness in the process. The reality, though, is that females outnumber males in college applicant pools. According to the National Student Clearinghouse, nearly 60 percent of the students in college in 2020–21 were women. This trend will probably continue, as there is also a decrease in the number of men enrolling in college. When you look at the gender difference among Black students, the balance becomes grossly lopsided, with often an 80 to 20 percent gender split among Black students. The disparity in gender at some HBCUs is much

Coppin State University (HBCU)
Baltimore, MD
1,800 Undergraduates
Private
Graduate Students: Yes
Setting: Urban

higher than at others with, for example, both Clark Atlanta University and Coppin State University having more than 75 percent female undergraduate enrollees. However, they are not alone, as many PWIs have a significant gender gap between male and female Black students, but these data are often not publicly reported. Thus, when it comes to admissions for Black female and male applicants, males would appear to have a decisive numbers advantage.

There Are More Black Men in Jail Than in College

As Black males growing up in the 1980s and 1990s, we always heard the perpetuated myth that "there are more Black men in jail than in college." Few things in my life have had the duality of being simultaneously great and frustrating as much as being a Black male. **Being a well-educated Black male has brought me praise, power, and position but also an acute awareness that all of it could be snatched away from me in a millisecond by someone who feels threatened by my color and gender**. All Black males in America deal with this in some way. Our parents, communities, and media often make us feel loved and revered as models of success in sports and entertainment. Still, too often we also learn to hate or undervalue ourselves. So much of what we see is hopelessness and despair that it can be impossible to ignore.

When we talk about Black males in the history of America, there is clearly a love-hate relationship. On one hand, Black men have long been revered as athletes, actors, civil rights leaders, and activists, but, on the other hand, they are often looked on as criminals and savages when viewed outside popular entertainment or politics. The idea of the Black man as an athlete is normalized, but a Black man who's an intellectual is something rarely seen. The reality, though, is that Black men have a far better chance of reaching long-term financial success with a college education or by entrepreneurship than they do of becoming a professional athlete.

An argument could be made that the most valuable group of people to higher education institutions is Black males. Consider the amount of revenue generated by college football and men's basketball through multibillion-dollar television contracts, which serve as the foundation of the National Collegiate Athletic Association (NCAA) and fund many of the other intercollegiate sports. In 2019 it was estimated that the NCAA generated almost twenty billion dollars in revenue, with Black males as the primary drivers behind it. As sought after as many young Black men are for their athletic talents, so too are the brightest Black males sought after at the top academic schools in the country for their academic abilities and the diversity they bring to campus. While there are many factors that go into recruiting for both athletics and academics, in both cases, the numbers don't lie. If you show a coach a football player who can run the 40-yard dash in 4.2 seconds or a basketball player with a 40-inch vertical jump who can shoot three-pointers, the coach is going to find it hard to pass on such rare ability. The same is true for a Black male with a 3.8 GPA and 1400 on the SAT or 34 on the ACT; not many schools are going to pass on that applicant either.

If you are a parent or guardian of a Black male, you are aware of the many challenges that Black males in America have faced through history and in the current climate. There has been much attention paid to the many deadly encounters between police and Black people in the past few years. Many Black parents have "the talk" early on with their sons and daughters about how they should conduct themselves when encountering the police. It's good to know that the college search process is one of the rare situations in society where Black males are held in high regard, and academically accomplished Black males have a distinct advantage over many of their fellow applicants. Black males make up one of the smallest populations in most college applicant pools, with only Native and Indigenous students being fewer in most instances. Because Black males make up such a small portion of applicants for many universities and colleges, they have become a high priority in many applicant pools.

Enrollment managers look at the makeup of the applicant pool and notice the small portion of Black males, as well as the subset of that small portion who are admissible. And because an even smaller subset than that will wind up enrolling, this population becomes even more important for schools looking to compose diverse classes. Given the shortage of Black male applicants, you will see news stories about a Black male who's admitted to all the Ivies. While it's a great accomplishment for this applicant, it highlights the priority that so many schools give to this population. A student can attend only one college at a time, of course. There is a period of time following admissions known as "yield season," when schools do all they can to get the top admitted students, not just Black students, to enroll. They pursue any number of methods, including fly-in programs that bring students from across the country to their campus to experience campus culture and hear pitches about academic programs, competitive financial aid packages and scholarships, and other incentives. Schools want these admitted students to enroll so that the schools can achieve their institutional priorities.

By no means are we saying that Black males are guaranteed admission by reason of simply applying, but they do occupy a unique place in higher education admissions by reason of their scarcity. I (Tim) can remember more than once coming across a Black man with a highly competitive application who was referred to as a "unicorn" in the applicant pool. You will hear coaches talk about a once-in-a-lifetime athlete who will change the game; well, that same conversation goes on in admissions offices throughout the country as well. **In both academics and athletics, postsecondary education puts a premium on Black males, but it is important that we define their needs and put their life success ahead of the needs of institutions that have not historically created spaces to support their identity and personal growth.**

Black Girl Magic

Black males have a numbers advantage in the admissions process, and Black females have a hard path to admission because of enrollment models. By the numbers, Black female applicants have better grades, test scores, extracurricular involvement, and application essays than Black males do. This is a sweeping generalization, we know, but there is an abundance of Black females competing in selective college admissions at the top universities in the country. The same cannot be said about their Black male counterparts. But this is nothing new; we all know that the foundation of Black America was built on the shoulders of Black women such as Harriet Tubman and Sojourner Truth and, in a later era, Shirley Chisholm (Brooklyn College) and Condoleezza Rice (University of Denver). It was a great moment when Barack Obama was elected the first Black president of the United States, but where would he have been without Oprah? And some would argue that Michelle is the more popular and revered Obama. The Black women who have made an impression on all facets of this country are countless, and recently there have been no bigger names than Vice President Kamala Harris and Stacey Abrams.

Brooklyn College (PWI)
Brooklyn, NY
11,000 Undergraduates
Public
Graduate Students: Yes
Setting: Urban

University of Denver (PWI)
Denver, CO
5,400 Undergraduates
Private
Graduate Students: Yes
Setting: Urban

Black women are the most educated population in the workplace, outpacing all other groups. Yet, on average, they are paid 35 percent less than white men and 15 percent less than white women, which gives truth to the saying "you have to work twice as hard to get half as far." As troubling as this is, there is an initiative by the company Goldman Sachs to help reduce disparities in pay. The company is making a ten-billion-dollar investment to address racial and gender bias in the workplace, with Black women being a major focus. This is good news for Black female college graduates who will be entering the workforce in the upcoming years, but the challenges for Black females begin long before that. They have one of the hardest challenges getting into the most selective schools in the country because they make up most of the applicant pool's Black students.

With around four thousand colleges and universities in the country, there are plenty of opportunities for young Black women to get a great education. But suppose your daughter is looking to attend any of the most selective colleges. In that case, it's going to take some "Black Girl Magic" to get in. Your daughter may have a 4.0 GPA, great test scores, and all the other accomplishments that make for a competitive candidate, but so will many other young Black females who'll apply. This is why you must ask questions during the college search: What makes my daughter special? What makes her different from other young women like her? What can she contribute to the school's community? And what school is going to appreciate what she has to offer?

In my more than twenty years in higher education, one of the hardest conversations I (Tim) ever had was telling one of my closest friends that her daughter was "regular" in the context of a selective college applicant pool. My friend shared with me all of her daughter's achievements with a great deal of pride, and they were truly great accolades; but the reality was that, in a selective college applicant pool, she would be put on a waitlist at best. At many other schools she would be a clear admit, but my friend wanted her daughter to go to a top-tier school, and in those schools' applicant pools, she would be just another "smart Black girl." This is disappointing and frustrating for all of us, but thankfully I was able to have this difficult conversation with her given our close friendship.

We want to make sure that the parents of daughters know this about the college admissions process: the numbers are not on their daughters' side in the way they are for sons. I (Tim) try to wrap my mind around this dynamic each day as I raise my twin son and daughter. They are just nine years old now, but it's obvious to see that, as with most children this age, my daughter "just gets it" while my son, equally as bright, gets the "he's a boy" pass, which many boys get throughout adolescence. Yes, I want both to strive for their best, but I must also deal with the reality of a society and educational world that will judge them differently, and I have already begun to teach them that "life is not fair." When we started in the profession, we had the naïve idea that the kids who were the smartest were the ones that were admitted, but over the past twenty-five years, we have witnessed firsthand that this is simply not true; the college admissions process is layered and has many nuances that make it difficult to understand from the outside looking in.

Sports, Arts, and Special Talents

Overview

All of our beautiful Black children are gifted. Whether they have talent in the arts, athletics, sciences, math, technology, or a host of other things, we know for sure that they are not just numbers on a transcript. Oftentimes our children are interested in attending a college that will augment their gifts. We all know that many Division I and II college athletes do not pay full tuition for their education. Especially in football and basketball, scholarships are offered to high school students who, a school believes, will help it win games. This chapter provides an overview of how college admissions works for students with recruitable talent that may yield a scholarship. We discuss some do's and don'ts for students who hope to be recruited for the arts or athletics.

If your child has talent in the visual or performing arts, they belong to a distinctive group of college applicants. As a parent, you have helped them hone their craft, probably spending loads of money on materials and lessons as well as sacrificing tremendous amounts of time. Now your child must decide if this craft they've developed will help them get into college and if they want to major in the arts.

To be considered a candidate in the arts, applicants frequently have to create a portfolio of work or prepare for an audition. For students to show their best work, they must know what to do and when to do it. Whether their talent is in music, dance, drama, studio art, or computer animation, what is critical are timing, research, and preparation.

Is Your Child Considering an
Art School or Conservatory?

If your child's ambition is to create art or perform for a living, then an art-intensive program is definitely the way to go. If, however, your child sees their art as a way to help them get into a school, but they (or you) are hesitant to commit to an art major, then maybe they should instead join a club, band, theater group, or use the studios available at the college they attend. Just as you would if your child were being recruited for athletics, you need to research the programs, professors, facilities, local venues, and internships available at schools of interest. One important question to ask is, What kind of degree should your child get? There are multiple possibilities: a BA (bachelor of arts), a BFA (bachelor of fine arts), or a BM (bachelor of music). There is no one degree that works for everyone.

What Are Visual and Performing Arts
Departments Looking For?

When it comes to recruiting art students, here are three things that almost always hold true:

1. Colleges want to see a student's current ability and range to determine if they have the potential to succeed in an art program.
2. Art programs want to see a student's individual style and creativity.
3. Admissions officers and faculty members for the visual and performing arts do consider grades and test scores; they just don't weight them as heavily as they do the portfolio or audition. Do not let your child think that their grades do not matter, however. What admissions officers are looking for are artistic talent and dedication *and* a solid academic record.

Can My Child Get a Scholarship for
Music, Dance, or Visual Art?

There are absolutely scholarships available to students in the arts. Many public and private colleges offer merit aid for students who will contribute to the artistic life of campus. However, to be clear, this can only happen if the student majors in the art. This cannot be a hobby if you expect scholarship money to be attached to it.

How Should My Child Prepare a
Portfolio or for an Audition?

Nothing is more important than knowing the requirements and deadlines for each college. Each school has strict guidelines that applicants must follow. The earlier that students start to gather artwork or record performances, the less rushed they will feel when it's time to present to a college. There are even "national portfolio days" when students and parents can meet with schools to present a student's work, and the student may get an offer of admission that day.

When your child is considering a performing arts school, you should evaluate it based on certain criteria. Here are a few questions to consider:

1. Is the school a conservatory or a university?
2. What majors are offered (a BFA or BA degree)?
3. How are the facilities (studios, practice rooms, equipment)?
4. Who are the key faculty members in the discipline of interest?
5. What art events happen at the school that your child would like to take part in?
6. Can your child pursue a double major or a major and minor in another department?
7. What is your child's specific area of interest within music, visual arts, dance, or theater? There are few generalists; most students who receive scholarships specialize in one area.

Does Your Child Want to Play a Sport in College?

In the last chapter, Tim wrote about Black men being the most valued asset on a college campus, oftentimes because of their participation in sports. Black men dominate in college football and college basketball. As I (Shereem) write this, I am thinking about Sam "Bam" Cunningham, who passed away in fall 2021. For those who do not know who he was, he was a running back at the University of Southern California and later in the NFL. Notably, Sam was a part of USC's "all Black" backfield—the first one of its kind in Division I (NCAA) history—that included quarterback Jimmy Jones and running back Clarence Davis. Sam had a remarkable debut performance (135 yards, two touchdowns) against an all-white University of Alabama football team, as USC beat Alabama 42 to 21 in Birmingham on September 12, 1970. Sam's performance in the game was reportedly a factor in convincing the University of Alabama and its fans to let Coach Bear Bryant integrate southern football. Jerry Claiborne, a former Bryant assistant, said, "Sam Cunningham did more to integrate Alabama in 60 minutes than Martin Luther King Jr. did in 20 years."

University of Alabama (PWI)
Tuscaloosa, AL
31,000 Undergraduates
Public
Graduate Students: Yes
Setting: Remote

We are all aware of the prominence of sports culture in America, and many of our Black children think of elite athletes as heroes and aim to emulate them on the field or on the court. Many affluent Black families owe their wealth to athletics. Whether athletics helped them get into college or they played a sport professionally, these Black athletes were smart with their money and used it as a foundation for wealth building. No one hates more than I do the assumption, which some people believe, that we were bred to be superior athletes through slavery. The notion that Blacks should "just dribble" or that we're so athletic but never cerebral infuriates me. However, it is a perception that is pervasive, and it passes down to our children, who are often praised, by us and others, for their athletic prowess more than their academic achievements.

I am a sports-obsessed dad who is fortunate to have a son who is equally as sports-obsessed. As a left-handed pitcher at the age of fifteen, he was offered a scholarship to play baseball by the University of North Carolina at Chapel Hill. Given what I saw as his potential as early as twelve years old, I knew he could play college baseball, and I have always encouraged his aspiration to play professionally. As a college advisor, I became keenly aware of how college recruiting for athletics works, how early it begins, and what we should do to help our children succeed. I added to my company's team an advisor who specializes in college sports recruiting.

Something happened, though, that changed my outlook. My son was asked to decommit from the team after a year and a half of belonging to the 2022 recruiting class at UNC–Chapel Hill. The school called him, not me, and told him that, due to COVID-19, there were too many kids on the team for him to play as a freshman. This was hard for a sixteen-year-old to hear but was even harder for me as a father to comprehend. The school didn't call me. It didn't call his high school coach. It called a child, and it was right then that I understood how cutthroat and cruel college recruiting can be.

I won't dwell on my disappointment but want instead to share what I learned. I know many other parents who trusted a coach's word and were then dropped unexpectedly. It happens to athletes of all colors. Thankfully, my son landed on his feet. If UNC had recruited him, then he would be recruited by another Power Five or equally strong program. But his rejection by UNC demonstrates how athletes are commoditized and expendable. If you want your child to be recruited or, better yet, if your child believes they have the talent to be recruited, you need to have your child evaluated by a credible coach or at a prospect camp or a showcase. Your child doesn't need to attend every single camp or showcase—they can get expensive—but you need to market your child if college coaches are trying to engage with them. The adage "if you're good enough, they will find you" is true in most cases, but as a parent involved in your child's college search, you'll want to identify what schools are best for your child athletically, academically, and socially. We should not jump hastily on the first opportunity that someone presents to us; instead we should survey the landscape and consider schools' cultures and how an experience and degree from a school will benefit our child.

Let me describe some possible steps to take for a family that's considering athletic recruitment as part of the admissions process.

Reclassing

Reclassing, or reclassifying, is holding a child back a year in middle school or high school so that they'll have an edge athletically by being taller, stronger, or more skilled than their peers. Parents are usually the ones who take the initiative in reclassing their child. Schools vary in their rules about whether an administrator has to sign off to permit a child to repeat a grade. But even when a principal has the right of refusal and doesn't allow reclassing, determined parents can take matters into their own hands and simply switch schools. Some have done just that.

> *"It's not because a kid is not doing well in school or is too young for his grade. It's just because you'll be one year older in high school, and you'll be that much better of a player."* (Bob Hurley, Hall of Fame basketball coach and head coach at St. Anthony's School in New Jersey)

Although my son did not reclass, despite being told that it would benefit his athletic development, I want more Black parents to be aware of reclassing. This practice is widespread for baseball among white families. Some call it "cheating"; others say it's the best and sometimes only way to get a Division I athletic scholarship. Many elite athletes in all sports are nineteen or twenty years old when they enter college. This is because they reclassed. It is a strategy that you should consider with some professional counsel from a coach or advisor you trust.

Schools Other Than Division I

Do not let ESPN make you think that the only students who get athletic scholarships play in the Power Five conferences (SEC, ACC, Pac-12, Big Ten, and Big 12). Plenty of HBCUs, Division II, and schools in the NAIA (National Association of Intercollegiate Athletics) offer athletic scholarships as well. Division III and Ivy League schools do not offer athletic scholarships, but they can recruit students and be creative with financial aid if they want an athlete badly enough. That's a secret they will not tell you in an information session.

Have a Resume and Video of
Your Child's Accomplishments

Make it easy for a recruitment coordinator to evaluate your child. If you share a resume and video (not only a highlight reel) with a coordinator, they have the choice to look at it or not. Many will discard it because they get so many of them, but someone will review it, and that person may want to recruit your child. Please encourage your child to go to a school where they are wanted—and will play—instead of where they will get the most initial recognition on social media.

Do Not Overlook HBCUs

Thankfully, and primarily due to Deion Sanders at Jackson State University, many elite high school athletes are rethinking what's important to them and are not just going where history has told them is the pathway to the pros. Many of the greatest NFL players—Shannon Sharpe (Savannah State), Jerry Rice (Mississippi Valley State University), Walter Payton (Jackson State University), and Steve McNair (Alcorn State University)—played football at HBCUs. We would be remiss if we did not also highlight celebrated sports journalist Pam Oliver, Florida A&M graduate, who has been covering the NFL and other sports for more than twenty years and has worked

Savannah State University (HBCU)
Savannah, GA
3,000 Undergraduates
Public
Graduate Students: Yes
Setting: Midsize City

Mississippi Valley State University (HBCU)
Bena, MS
1,700 Undergraduates
Public
Graduate Students: Yes
Setting: Remote

Alcorn State University (HBCU)
Lorman, MS
2,700 Undergraduates
Public
Graduate Students: Yes
Setting: Remote

closely with many of the greats. Many great NBA players came from HBCUs as well: Ben Wallace (Virginia Union University), Charles Oakley (Virginia Union University), and Anthony Mason (Tennessee State University). Identifying what school, whether it is a PWI or an HBCU, is going to give your child the best chance to realize their dreams is what should drive the college search process. I am a strong believer that HBCUs, especially for football and basketball, should be considered for young men who have aspirations of playing professionally.

Fun fact about Tim: He earned a cross-country and track scholarship while at Morehouse that he did not have when he matriculated. He made the team as a walk-on and proved himself to be such a valuable contributor to the team that he was offered scholarship money as an athlete for his sophomore, junior, and senior years, winning multiple championships along the way. Isn't that cool!

Contact Coaches

"A closed mouth can't get fed." That saying is true in business and in college recruiting. If your child wants to attend a certain school, they must reach out to it. There are recruitment questionnaires online to fill out, and there are opportunities for students to take the initiative to connect with coaches. Given how much time an athlete spends with a team and its coach, many athletes choose the coach more than they choose the school. Of course, coaches may leave for a new job, but do not underestimate how important a coach is to your child's college recruitment and college experience.

Should Parents Reach Out to Coaches?

I have reached out to coaches and introduced myself when I think my son may be a good fit for a school. When I have allowed my son to be the sole contact with a coach, I have kicked myself: coaches have an agenda, and I will no longer allow my child—he's not eighteen years old and he's still on my dime—to navigate adult situations alone. Some people may disagree with this approach, and some coaches may be turned off by parental involvement. But I am a kind and courteous person, and I want to see if someone that I may entrust with my son is kind and courteous as well.

Many Black parents want their student-athletes to play at the highest level they can and to be funded to do so. There are some myths out there about athletic scholarships that we need to address.

Myth: Athletic scholarships are full rides offered in the senior year of high school.
Not true. In fact, most athletic scholarships are partial (or equivalency) scholarships, as each team's coach has a limited number of scholarships to offer each entering class. Other than football and basketball—the biggest athletic money generators for most institutions—only Division I tennis, gymnastics, and volleyball can offer full-ride scholarships for athletics. In recruiting athletes, a college coach can make a verbal offer as early as middle school, but it usually happens during freshman, sophomore, or junior year of high school, depending on the sport and the athlete's ability.

Please note the word *verbal*. In marital wedlock, vows matter, but a signed marriage certificate matters more. Students need to sign a National Letter of Intent to be officially committed to a school, and that happens during senior year. In our social media–driven world, too much is made of offers and verbal commitments. Do not believe that recruitment is secured until the ink is dry on the signed letter.

Myth: Talented athletes can get into any school even if their grades are poor.
Unfortunately, there is some truth to this one. Athletes are not held to the same admissions expectations at many elite universities, but your son or daughter should not think they can get Cs and Ds in

high school and then get into college with no problem. Recruitment depends on how much a coach wants them and will push for them in the admissions process. By the same token, a coach can look at a student's GPA and test scores and immediately be turned off given the seeming lack of effort or ability. Coaches want to invest in student-athletes who will do well in the classroom and graduate. They can then boast about that fact to the parents of their next recruit. I urge you not to let your child get lackadaisical in the classroom. Grades, test scores, character, and effort all matter. In some cases, including my son's, his test scores helped to boost his athletic scholarship offer because the coach pulled from other university funding sources adjacent to the athletic scholarship's allotment.

Coaches Need to Keep Their Promises

I don't want to paint a negative picture of all college coaches, but I want you to heed the warning in what happened to my son. Coaches' loyalty lies with themselves and their athletic program, not with your child. As happens frequently in college football, coaches leave schools, or are fired, with little warning and perhaps with little regard for who else is affected. Now your child must impress a new coach who did not recruit them. This is a troubling but real possibility. When coaches make offers to student-athletes, they often make more offers than they need to, knowing that every kid they offer a scholarship to may not choose their program. This form of over-recruiting by coaches makes recruitment risky for families. The best advice I can give on this is to ask any and every question you have. Try to get to know the coach's character. You are trusting another adult to help shepherd your child into adulthood. You need to partner with this person, and they need to be a contact in your phone. You need to make sure everyone is on the same page. I am not talking about a promise of playing time; I am talking about learning what the coach believes in, what their team's graduation rate is, and what former student-athletes are now doing with their lives. Most of all you, the parent, need to be confident that this person can be an additional life coach for your child.

Other Special Talents

Instead of arts *or* athletics, why not combine the two and get recruited? Colleges can offer scholarships for marching band and cheerleading, which support the athletic programs. The recruiting process for cheerleading is a little different from recruitment for other sports because it isn't a sanctioned NCAA sport, meaning that there are no established regulations around coach contact or recruiting calendars. Therefore, coaches and recruits can communicate and express interest at any time.

The key to earning most marching band scholarships is to be admitted to the school and, once admitted, to make the band. If your child is interested in a particular school, see if the school has a summer band camp. This experience can improve their performing, raise their profile as a marching band performer, and give them a feel for the school's band and its band director.

We must continue to celebrate our children for all their gifts and use their gifts to get funding for college. Money is probably the greatest obstacle to all Black children getting a college education. Historically, the arts and athletics have helped us fund what we all deserve. We encourage you to help your child maximize their potential for whatever they aspire to be and to identify colleges and scholarships, for athletics or arts, that ultimately best suit their needs.

CHAPTER 10

Show Me the Money

Overview

College is expensive; there is no way around it. As families begin to think about college, funding an education should be at the forefront of the conversation. Financial aid offers will vary for each family. We do not get into the granular aspects of how aid packages are created because that is not our area of expertise; instead, we provide an overview of what families need to know as they think about how to fund their child's education. We also define financial aid terms.

———————

Getting into college is one thing, but paying for college is a completely different challenge, especially given the continuing rising cost of tuition. When it comes to financial aid, students and families echo the words of Cuba Gooding Jr.'s character in *Jerry Maguire*— "Show me the money!" Paying for higher education is like taxes: everyone is going to have to pay some amount for college, but how much someone will pay depends on many factors.

At most colleges and universities, the financial aid process is separate from the admissions process. It is also more complex than most people realize. Federal, state, and institutional aid award amounts are determined and overseen by formulas. Oftentimes financial aid professionals can explain the formulas, but they have little control over how much money is allocated to students. Some financial aids packages are filled with loans instead of merit aid and grants. Why? Because most colleges cannot afford to meet 100 percent of all students' actual need.

Federal direct student loans are entitlements that allow US citizens and those with a Permanent Resident Card to borrow funds for college costs from the US Department of Education. These loans do not require credit checks or a creditworthy cosigner, which makes them relatively easy to get but also dangerous. We encourage families to read the fine print of a loan's terms and try to understand them as best they can. Many of us do not see loans as a form of financial aid because they have to be repaid. That is why students need a plan in place for getting a job after graduation that will let them begin repaying their loans as quickly as possible.

We would advise everyone to apply for financial aid, no matter how well off your family is. If you don't apply for aid, there is little to no chance of receiving anything. We often hear from families who were told or who assume they would not qualify for financial aid given how much money they make. There are schools that award aid for reasons other than need and merit; if students don't have an aid application on file, however, they are not considered for some of these additional funding opportunities.

Another important reason for families to apply for aid is the fact that you never know what may happen to your finances. Having been in higher education through a recession and a global pandemic that affected almost all families financially in some way, we have witnessed firsthand how colleges and universities were able to step in and supplement funding for students who had aid applications on file. We encourage all families to apply for aid, but ultimately applying is a personal decision. Please note that requirements vary from school to school, but many schools are going to require most, if not all, of the forms and documentation we describe later in the chapter. **Always remember: the college or university is the best resource for information about the financial aid process for your child.**

Adhere to *all* deadlines. Deadlines are one of the most important parts of the admissions process. Missing them can cost your student the chance to apply to schools as well as access to financial aid.

Without timely submission of financial aid information, students will be unable to receive an aid package. Thus, it is imperative that parents and guardians submit all aid documents by the deadlines because in many instances financial aid, especially institutional, is awarded on a first-come, first-served basis. If you miss deadlines, often the remaining amount of aid available will be limited. We cannot impress upon families and guardians enough the importance of submitting aid documents ahead of deadlines.

Preparing to Pay for College

There are steps you should take as early as possible in preparation for funding your child's education:

Begin talking about money as early as possible. Having candid family conversations about the cost of higher education is critical. Both parents and student need to manage expectations around college choices based on the family's income and savings.

Consider the option of opening a 529 savings plan. A 529 plan is a tax-advantaged savings plan designed to encourage saving for future education costs. These plans, legally known as "qualified tuition plans," are sponsored by states, state agencies, or educational institutions and are authorized by section 529 of the Internal Revenue Code. By opening a 529 savings plan, you will be able to save money toward your child's college education, and you will also receive some tax deductions in most states. You can also use your 529 assets for K–12 tuition up to $10,000 per student per year at a public, private, or religious school. If this is of interest to you, contact your accountant or tax professional.

Use a net price calculator (NPC). Net price calculators are available on colleges' and universities' websites. They allow prospective students to enter information about themselves to find out what students like them paid to attend the institution the previous year, after taking grants and scholarship aid into account. If the NPC determines there's a difference in the cost of the school and what your family can pay, you will need to apply for aid and review the information we provide in the remainder of this chapter.

Be prepared to pay something. A full scholarship by which a family pays no money at all for their student to attend college for four years is rare. Even if your child does receive a scholarship, you should have some money set aside for incidental costs and emergencies.

Be prepared to apply for aid annually. Your family will have to go through this process every year that your student is enrolled in college.

Financial Aid 101

Applying for financial aid today is not the same process that it was for those of us who went to college decades ago. More than likely you will never touch a piece of paper. Everything today is digital. Your child will probably not have to wait for hours to see a financial aid counselor; in fact they may never meet their financial aid counselor. There is so much about the process that has changed, but there are a lot of things that have stayed the same. Below are some terms you need to know.

Applying for Aid

There are two applications you will need to complete if you are applying for financial aid:

FAFSA (Free Application for Federal Student Aid). The FAFSA is a form that current and prospective college students complete in the United States to determine their eligibility for student financial aid. The FAFSA is different from the CSS Profile, which some colleges also require. Students must submit this form to be eligible for federal financial aid, including grants, loans, and work-study. Parents should help students complete it to ensure the accuracy of the information since it is the dominant financial resource for college students. There is a federal method for determining the expected family contribution, or EFC. The FAFSA should be submitted, ideally, in October of the student's twelfth-grade year. As its name suggests, this is a *free* application, so you should never pay to submit it.

CSS Profile. The College Board's CSS Profile is an online application that collects information used by hundreds of colleges, universities, professional schools, and scholarship programs to award financial aid from sources outside the federal government. It is found on the College Board's website (www.collegeboard.org) and is often required in addition to the FAFSA. Each college has a different method for calculating financial need. This application must be filed in October of a student's senior year. This application will primarily be required by private and some larger public schools to help award merit and non-federal aid. Currently, more than four hundred schools require this additional application. The reason that schools ask for this additional application is to have a better understanding of the resources available to support students when the schools are giving out millions of dollars in institutional aid.

When you complete these forms, you will need to have your tax return prepared and available. With any financial aid application, tax returns are necessary for documenting finances. Recent updates to aid regulations allow families to use prior year tax returns, meaning they can use 2021 tax returns if applying for aid in 2023, but up-to-date tax returns are more helpful for schools trying to put together the best aid package. Don't worry about needing any paper copies. Technology has made it possible to have your most recent tax returns sent to the school directly from the federal government without leaving the FAFSA or CSS Profile sites.

Another important part of financial aid is having a complete understanding of your family's financial situation. Financial aid offices are aware that there are families where parents are divorced or where students are in foster care or where a student's guardians have died. No matter the situation, it is critical that all adults who provide financial support to a college-bound student furnish tax documents to financial aid offices.

One request that an aid office often makes is for submission of a non-custodial waiver form. This form allows families to provide additional information about a parent or guardian who does not live with the student to determine if tax information from that individual can be waived. Aid offices will make that determination in such instances.

The FAFSA, CSS Profile, and your tax documents are used to determine your family's demonstrated/calculated financial need. To calculate your family's demonstrated need, the school will take the cost of attendance and subtract from it your family's expected family contribution.

Expected family contribution (EFC). Determined by the FAFSA using the federal method and reported to the family in the Student Aid Report. The EFC determines need-based federal and state aid as well as aid from many colleges. The EFC represents the minimum amount that a family is expected to contribute toward college expenses in a given year. Merit and need-based aid do not reduce the EFC.

Cost of attendance (college sticker price). The direct billable costs (tuition and fees, room and board) and indirect costs (books, supplies, personal expenses). This can vary from family to family depending on spending habits.

Most colleges do not meet 100 percent of demonstrated financial need, creating a gap, which is the pressure point for many families in paying for college. Once your demonstrated need is determined, a financial award offer is put together for your student. In this award, financial aid comes in four primary forms: scholarships (need-based and merit-based), grants, work-study, and student loans. Let's define each.

Merit-based scholarships. These are awarded for achievements and skills, including academic excellence, athletic or artistic ability, or volunteer service. This type of scholarship is often awarded immediately following high school or during college. There are multiple resources to learn about scholarships, and we suggested some in the introduction. We also recommend that you read *The Ultimate Scholarship Book* by Gen and Kelly Tanabe.

Need-based scholarships. These are awarded in cases of financial necessity. These scholarships are awarded according to a family's income, liabilities, savings, and assets.

Grants. These are funds given to your child that do not need to be paid back. Most grants are based on financial need calculated with the FAFSA; they come from the state or the federal government and are awarded through a college. Federal Pell Grants can be awarded in an amount over $5,000. Private and some public universities have additional institutional grants they can award apart from federal or state grants.

Work-study. This is a job your student is hired for at the college; they qualify for work-study employment through demonstrated need as determined by the financial aid office. Jobs can take place at many spots on campus, such as working in a library, a dining hall, or an administrative office. These jobs offer students a paycheck during college so they can have pocket money or put it toward their tuition bill. Work-study aid is a part of a financial award, but students must work to receive it.

Loans. Yes, we know *loan* is a four-letter word. For students and parents to take out loans is not ideal, but often it is necessary. The goal of taking out any loan should be an investment in a student's potential future earnings. The key is to borrow as little as possible—by parent or student—and to pay it back as quickly as possible. We do not recommend taking out private student loans because of the higher interest rates and because the expectation usually is that they will need to be paid back soon.

Below are some important terms to know when discussing loans:

Interest rate. An expense charged for borrowing money. The percentage of the interest rate varies.

Subsidized loan. A direct federal loan based on need. Interest does not accrue while a student is in college.

Unsubsidized loan. A direct federal loan not based on need. Interest does accrue while a student is in college.

Master Promissory Note. A legally binding contract you must sign when accepting any kind of federal loan. This outlines all the terms and conditions under which you agree to repay the loan.

Consolidation loan note. This combines all direct federal student loans into a single loan with one lender and one interest rate.

Parent PLUS loan. A direct federal loan to parents or graduate students that has a higher interest rate than undergraduate student loans.

Perkins Loan. A loan directly from a college rather than the federal government, one awarded for exceptional financial need.

We just covered a lot of terminology pertaining to financial aid. The reality is that financial aid is one of the most complicated parts of college admissions. Aid offices do all they can to provide as much financial support to students as institutional funding allows. When families begin the process of applying for financial aid, they must know the importance of submitting the appropriate documentation, meeting all deadlines, and following up with aid offices to complete the process. We would encourage families not to be defensive or secretive about submitting financial information, as aid offices are not asking for your financial information for any reason other than to provide the best aid package for your student. They want to *show you the money*.

Facts about the FAFSA and Financial Aid

Since the FAFSA collects the principal information for all financial aid awards, we offer you some facts that should help you complete it well.

1. The official FAFSA website is www.fafsa.ed.gov. ONLY USE THIS WEBSITE! You should *never* pay to complete the FAFSA.
2. Federal financial aid, like most state and university aid, is available on a first-come, first-served basis. The sooner you get your application in, the better your chances will be of qualifying. Deadlines are very important.
3. Accept money in this order:
   - Free money (scholarships and grants)
   - Earned money (work-study)
   - Borrowed money (loans)
4. After registering for the FAFSA, you will receive an FSA ID. This expires every eighteen months. Parents can use their FSA ID when completing the FAFSA application for multiple dependents.
5. Each FSA ID must be tied to a separate email address. Parents and child cannot use the same email address.
6. There is a tool called the IRS Data Tool that saves you time when filling out the FAFSA because tax information is taken directly from the IRS's database and populated in your FAFSA. You're less likely to make mistakes using this, and you will not need to manually gather your tax records before applying.
7. If a major life event impacts your finances, but is not reflected in your FAFSA (job loss, family illness, personal illness), contact the financial aid office at the schools to which your child is applying and have your records updated. Sometimes schools can make accommodations given the new circumstances.

8. When does a student *not* need their parents' financial information to qualify for federal or institutional financial aid?
    - If the student is twenty-four years or older by December 31 of the school year for which they are applying for financial aid
    - Is working toward a master's or doctorate degree
    - Is married
    - Is currently serving in the US military as active duty

Parents, before you pass judgment on student loans, ask yourself two questions about your own loans: (1) Would I be where I am in life without those loans? (2) Did I use those loans responsibly?

Let your answers frame how you see the use of loans in your child's higher education, if they are to be a part of your child's financial aid package.

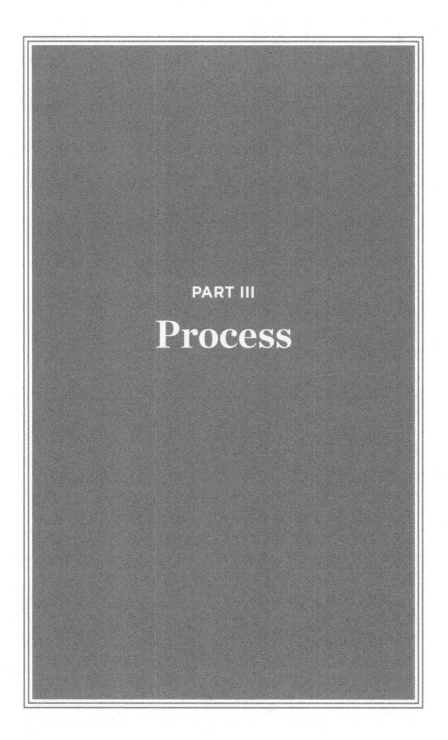

PART III

Process

CHAPTER 11

Expectation for Success Timeline

Overview

In this chapter, we discuss when the college search should begin, areas to focus on as your family puts your college list together, and important things to consider to limit anxiety. In college admissions, there is a context for why we do what we do and things that are necessary to understand in order to succeed during the search and when applying. What we have in common with families of other races are the timeline, policies, and procedures of the college admissions process. Some rules and requirements must be adhered to regardless of whether you are applying to PWIs or HBCUs. We explain the application process so that you and your child will understand what will be expected of you. This process must be intentionally managed and executed in order for your child to have college admissions success.

The college application process has many moving parts. Its foundational components may be similar to what they were twenty to thirty years ago, but the changes that the process has undergone and the strategies your child needs to employ to better their chances of being admitted should not be underestimated.

Overwhelmingly in our interviews and roundtable discussions with Black parents, most assumed the process started during or at the end of the eleventh grade, or even worse, some said senior year. This is not true. The process has to start much earlier than that. It must start with students choosing the right classes in the ninth grade. This lays the foundation for possible honors, advanced, Advanced Placement, or International Baccalaureate courses later in high school. In tenth grade, they'll be on a trajectory where they can start to consider selective universities based on the classes they're taking. During the ninth and tenth grades, they can also get involved in extracurricular activities and gradually become leaders. Around the same time, they can take diagnostic standardized tests to determine which test may be better for them. This is just a snapshot of the steps students should take early in their high school experience. It was hard for us to hear school counselor interviewees, Black and white, tell us that Black parents are too often "late to the game" or not engaged enough in the college preparation process. Those who are best prepared and armed with information early will win the game when it's time.

Throughout this book we have emphasized how the college admissions process is individualized and specific to every student and family, so we find it difficult to give definite answers to questions such as these:

1. When should a family begin the college search process?
2. How many colleges should a student apply to?
3. What are the chances of the student getting into a particular college?

Our answer most of the time is "it depends," especially when it comes to selective colleges and universities, both PWIs and HBCUs. We sometimes have a parent or counselor tell us what they heard about why a student was admitted or was not admitted to a school in an effort to draw a comparison with another student. In most instances, though, there are few similarities shared by any two applicants. So, our first bit of advice is to take information you hear from others about the college admissions process with a grain of salt, because there is no formula that guarantees admission.

We are not going to tell you what type of school your student should be looking at, but we do think it is important to provide some guidance that will help parents and students when they think about building a college list. Given the differences in our experiences, I (Tim) will come at the process from the "macro" view of a college admissions officer, and Shereem will examine it from a "micro" view given his experience working directly with students and families as a college counselor and consultant.

Once students get a sense of the schools they want to apply to, they may be interested in a school their family cannot afford. I am a big proponent of having that conversation early on in the process to manage expectations. In our experience, a lot of the anxiety can be mitigated with open communication about cost and what resources are available to fund the student's education.

Currently, many schools are touting being test-optional, but the reality is that standardized testing remains an important part of admissions for the foreseeable future. Near the end of their sophomore year, students should begin to think about testing and have a sense of how well they have tested in the past in order to decide whether they will need test prep going into their junior year. I would recommend that students take a diagnostic version of the SAT or ACT to find out how well they do; the results will help the family formulate a plan going into the student's senior year. Families may determine that it's best to apply only to test-optional schools, get some test prep to improve the student's scores, or change the schools the student will apply to based on their score. No matter what, we encourage all students to take the SAT or ACT at least once, particularly if they intend to apply for scholarships.

As students enter their senior year, that is the time to firm up their college list and identify scholarship opportunities. Students should narrow down their list to eight to twelve schools. Some families may choose to apply to more schools than that, but in our professional opinion, having more than fifteen schools demonstrates a student's lack of focus. In addition, without fee waivers or using the Common Black College Application, which has a one-time fee of twenty dollars to apply to participating schools, submitting college applications can become expensive. Selective PWI college application fees frequently range from fifty to one hundred dollars. By no means are we telling you how to spend your money, but we want you to be smart about it given the cost of higher education and the low admit rate at many selective institutions.

The next part of the process is connecting with schools and asking questions specific to your college needs. At this time students should have a good sense of what they want out of their college experience. In the summer before their senior year and in the fall, students should formally engage with college admissions advisors and ask questions. Colleges and universities expect their admissions officers to meet virtually with students online via Zoom, or prior to the pandemic, officers used to travel around the country and the world to connect with prospective applicants. I (Tim) always offer my email and phone number as a resource to students whom I meet and invite them to ask me further questions when they have them. Sadly, too few students and families take advantage of the offer. Admissions officers are your best informational resource for the admissions process, so please connect with them and take advantage of the information they can share.

Tim and I (Shereem) chose to write this book together, not only because we both have extensive admissions experience but also because we have different opinions. This makes for spirited discussions (occasionally arguments) that let us hear (hopefully) the other person's points and decide whether to accept them. I do not share Tim's view that the college search should start in the ninth grade. I would say seventh grade, and I can even argue for third grade. That's because I come from an independent school background, where college awareness started before children could read. I read in an article in *Los Angeles* magazine that the esteemed Buckley School once had a sign at the school's entrance that read, "College begins at two," a favorite saying of Isabelle Buckley, who founded the K–12 school in 1933. The school boasts 100 percent college acceptance for its graduates.

The classes your child takes in middle school, especially in math, sciences, and foreign languages, affect the classes they will take in high school. This influences how rigorous their classes are and how selective universities will determine if they are prepared to handle the university's curriculum. Which classes your child takes matter a lot; this cannot be overstated. If your child wants to attend an elite PWI or HBCU, they must have a rigorous curriculum in high school, and they must do well in that rigorous curriculum.

The college admissions process begins with awareness in elementary school; setting an academic foundation begins in middle school; and an aspirational and action-oriented approach happens in high school. Over the years, your family should ask your child the questions below, and you should expect to hear evolving and gradually more mature responses.

- What is college?
- Why do people go?
- What happens there?
- What is the goal?

If we have conversations about these questions with our children in elementary school, they can begin to do their own research and then take appropriate courses and participate in extracurricular activities. College preparation is called a *process* for a reason. There are clear steps for students and parents to take that will make the process more manageable.

Timeline for Success: Grades Nine to Twelve

Please review this checklist with your child and adjust it as is appropriate for their aspirations and learning style.

Ninth Grade—Students

1. Get adjusted to high school academically and get the best grades possible.

2. Start exploring what extracurricular activities are offered (clubs, sports, community service, fine and performing arts).

3. Start to document activities, academic and extracurricular accomplishments, summer and work experiences.

4. Focus on time management skills: When will you do homework? How much time does it take you to complete homework thoroughly? What are you doing with your free time?

5. Discuss summer opportunities (e.g., a job or a summer course) with your school counselor and parents, and research them on your own.

Ninth Grade—Parents

- Have you discussed paying for college with your child? How much money have you saved? What is the budget?
- Questions to ask a school counselor:
  - Do ninth graders take the PSAT?
  - What is the sequence of courses to take that will lead to honors, advanced, or Advanced Placement (AP) courses later in high school?
  - How can my child take those classes and when?
  - When should my child visit or virtually connect with schools to demonstrate interest?

Tenth Grade—Students

1. Complete a personality or strength-finders assessment to learn more about your strengths, interests, and possible majors and careers. This will help with course selection.

2. Continue to explore extracurricular activities and start to think about possible leadership positions.

3. Update your documented activities and accomplishments list. This will become the basis for a resume.

4. Grades start to really matter, so you should be working hard and learning what subjects you like and excel in. You'll want

to take honors, advanced, and AP courses, if possible. Meet with your school counselor and a college admissions expert to discuss your plans.

5. Take the PSAT, if offered (in the fall).
6. Take a practice SAT and ACT (in the spring) to determine which one is better for you.
7. Be sure to use your summer productively and have a plan to work, volunteer, or do a project.
8. Start to research and build a list of colleges that you're interested in (see below).

Tenth Grade—Parents

- Schedule a local college visit or one while on vacation so that you can start to familiarize your child with different schools.
- Discuss possible majors and careers with your child using their personality and strength-finders assessment as the primary source of information.

How to Build a College List

There are four core factors to consider when creating a college list:

1. Cost
2. Location
3. Possible major
4. Possible career

Start with these and then add other factors that matter to your family. Parents need to be clear with students about how cost and location may bear on the choice of colleges. Students should have taken a personality, strength-finders, or career assessment to assist them in identifying possible majors and careers. Here are other factors to consider:

Size of school and size of academic departments that your child is interested in. Size affects how many courses are offered. Are professors accessible if a student needs additional help?

Academic reputation: Do college experts perceive this to be a "good school?" What is the ROI (return on investment)? (collegefactual.com) Does this college set students up for success after graduation?

How diverse is the student body racially, culturally, geographically, and socioeconomically?

What kinds of students are on campus? Percentages of Black students, white students, Latinx students, Asian and Pacific Islanders, Native and Indigenous, and international students?

What is the four-year graduation rate?

What is the average class size?

What are the housing and dining options?

How selective is the school (that is, hard to get into), and should you even apply if the school has a low acceptance rate?

How safe is the campus? What is the school's relationship with local law enforcement?

Are there fraternities and sororities? Is that important?

Are there religious services on campus? Are students required to attend?

What are the social and extracurricular activity opportunities on campus?

Do sports or Greek life dominate the social experience on weekends?

What is there to do off campus?

What kinds of job, career, or entrepreneurial preparation happens at the school?

Eleventh Grade—Students

This is the most important year of high school for college admissions preparation. Set clear academic goals and work hard. You are at the point when you must be aware of who you are and what's important to you and get excited about exploring all the possibilities that colleges offer.

Fall

1. Review your social media accounts and pay attention to what you post. *Nothing is private in social media*, and colleges may review the social media accounts of prospective students.
2. Review personality and strength-finders assessment, and take it again if necessary.
3. Start the year off strong; review your transcript and junior-year schedule. Are you taking honors, advanced, or AP courses?
4. Register for and take standardized tests (PSAT, ACT, or SAT).
5. Continue to invest yourself in extracurricular activities and seek out positions of leadership.
6. Start to visit colleges on school holidays, preferably when college students are on campus. (Ask school counselor about getting excused absences for these visits.)
7. Pay close attention to twelfth graders and their college application process.
8. Prepare for fall college visits (by coming up with questions to ask, etc.).
9. Ask a school counselor if you can join in-school college information sessions.

Eleventh Grade—Parents

- Attend a financial aid and college scholarship workshop or webinar.
- Schedule college visits.

Winter

1. Start to investigate summer opportunities and apply for programs, jobs, and internships.
2. Continue to research colleges, build your list, and visit campuses.
3. Register for senior-year courses and consider how specific courses will influence your application. Are you taking honors, advanced, or AP courses? In subjects or majors you want to pursue in college?

Eleventh Grade—Parents

- Review your family calendars for opportunities to visit schools.
- Schedule a meeting with a school counselor and attend school-sponsored college admissions workshops.

Spring

1. Discuss your college list with your school counselor with reference to your present transcript, test scores, and activities.
2. Start filling out college applications. (Most schools will use the Common Application, Coalition Application, or Common Black College Application, but some schools will have their own application.)
3. Brainstorm in response to application essay prompts.
4. Ask teachers for college recommendation letters.
5. Become a leader in your extracurricular activity for the upcoming twelfth grade, revise your resume, and add *all* high school activities.
6. Take the ACT or SAT and decide how many more times, if any, you need to retake it.
7. Plan to visit colleges.
8. Confirm summer plans.
9. Confirm senior-year class schedule.
10. Attend college fair or college information sessions to connect with admissions officers.

11. Discuss possibly applying Early Decision or Early Action.

12. Start to demonstrate interest to top colleges on your list (opening emails, following their social media accounts, attending virtual information sessions, engaging with admissions offices).

13. Be sure to submit what your high school guidance counselor asks of you ahead of all deadlines.

14. Attend any essay and application workshops offered by your high school.

Eleventh Grade—Parents

Questions to ask a school counselor:

- Can my child meet with college admissions representatives in their junior year when the representatives visit in person or virtually in the fall?
- When should we start to visit campuses virtually on our own?
- When is the junior-year college information presentation?
- Do you have any sample case studies of applicants for us to review?
- Is there a list of graduates from this high school who would be willing to speak with us about their experience at institutions of interest to us?
- What information goes into the school counselor recommendation?
- Do you read the teacher recommendations before they are sent?
- Can we see the school profile that you send to colleges?
- How often will we be able to meet with you?

Summer (between Eleventh and Twelfth Grades)

1. Relax and rejuvenate.

2. Enjoy your resume-building summer courses and activities.

3. Refine your college list after reviewing your final grades from junior year.

4. Research the types of applications, requirements, and deadlines that colleges and universities have.

5. Begin to draft your personal and supplemental essays, if you have not already.
6. Continue to work on the Common Application.
7. Register for virtual information sessions and interviews.
8. Continue with standardized test prep, if necessary.
9. Visit more colleges.

Late Summer (August)

1. The Common Application "rolls over" and can be submitted as early as August 1.
2. Start the Coalition Application, if necessary.
3. Revise personal statement and supplemental essays.
4. Register for interviews, if applicable.
5. Ask summer employers or mentors for an additional recommendation, if applicable.
6. Continue with standardized test prep, if necessary.
7. Take standardized test, if applicable.

Twelfth Grade—Students

Early Fall (September)

1. Finalize college list.
2. Keep track of all deadlines, applications completed, and what you have submitted to colleges.
3. Attend college informational sessions in person or online.
4. Discuss Early Decision and Early Action strategies.
5. Revise personal statement and supplemental essays.
6. Register for interviews, if applicable.
7. Proofread all Early Action and Early Decision applications and essays.
8. Take standardized tests for the last time, if applicable.
9. Actively look for scholarships.
10. Follow up with all recommendation writers.
11. Be sure to submit all the documents your high school guidance counselor asks for.

Twelfth Grade—Parents

- Complete the FAFSA (Free Application for Federal Student Aid).
- Meet with a high school counselor to understand their timeline, expectations, and procedures.
- Review (but do not revise) your student's essay(s) and share feedback.
- Proofread all of your student's essays and applications.

Fall (October and November)

1. Complete and submit all Early Action or Early Decision applications.
2. Complete and submit applications for all schools requiring a portfolio.
3. Have Early Action and Early Decision interviews, if applicable.
4. Ask a school counselor if and when your first quarter grades are being sent to your Early Action / Early Decision schools, if applicable.
5. Finalize regular decision college list and complete applications and essays.
6. Review application(s) submissions and interview deadlines for regular decision.
7. Begin to apply for scholarships.

Twelfth Grade—Parents

- Confirm that all financial aid information has been submitted.

Winter (December and January)

1. Discuss Early Decision II strategies, if applicable.
2. Regular decision and Early Decision II applications are generally due on or around January 1. Submit them in mid-December so that everyone can have a relaxing holiday break.

Winter (January–March)

1. If your Early Decision application is deferred by a college that you want to attend, correspond with the college and indicate that it is still a top choice. Offer any updates on activities, awards, and accomplishments.
2. Learn more about financing a college education over four years by attending workshops.
3. Beware of senioritis! This is when seniors get too comfortable and do not finish their senior year strong. This can lead to admission offers being rescinded or to being put on academic probation as a freshman in college.
4. Wait for application decisions.

Spring (March and April)

1. Receive decisions from schools and evaluate admission and financial aid options.
2. Visit colleges that you've been accepted to and are considering.
3. If waitlisted, consider remaining on the list and communicating with the school that you will attend, if this is in fact true.
4. Attend accepted students' receptions when possible.
5. Make a final decision and submit a deposit by May 1.

Spring (May)

1. Celebrate College Signing Day! Wear a shirt with your new school's name on it.
2. Notify your school counselor and any scholarships of your final decision.
3. Have your final transcript sent.
4. Sign up for campus housing.
5. Join freshmen social media groups to find a roommate.

CHAPTER 12

What Are Colleges Looking For?

Overview

Each college has different admissions requirements and selection criteria, but the principles we describe in this chapter are consistent with selective college admissions. If you follow them, we are confident that your child will be successful in the college search and application processes.

———

Every college your child applies to will want to see the three-to-four-year track record of the classes they took and the grades they got in them. In other words, **the most important part of your child's application is their transcript**. Colleges are looking for students who have shown that they want to learn and were engaged over four years and challenged themselves with an array of courses. For your child to be considered by a selective university, HBCU or PWI, **they must have taken a rigorous high school curriculum that includes honors, Advanced Placement, dual enrollment, or International Baccalaureate courses, if possible**. For those who attended a school that offers these courses and chose not to take them, they're putting themselves at a disadvantage.

Getting high grades in hard courses helps students get into selective schools. GPAs and class rank matter for most colleges in their admissions. Colleges want applicants to show they are eager and capable students who got good grades in high school. Yet, in some instances, receiving slightly lower grades in a rigorous curriculum is preferable to receiving all As in less challenging classes.

Please note, though, that there are degrees of selectivity. Some colleges, PWIs and HBCUs, will not accept students with a B average, which is roughly a 3.0 GPA. There are exceptions, of course, but they are rare among the most selective schools in the country. Each college publishes GPA averages for admission. The expectations are not written in stone, but you and your child should be aware of them, and your child's GPA should fall within the published range. All colleges have institutional priorities for what sorts of students they want to or need to admit each year. What does that mean? It means that college admissions offices are in the business of admitting a class, not necessarily a student. They take students who will make the class diverse and whole.

The Role of the College or School Counselor

The role of the school or college counselor is to support, guide, and serve as a partner with the family through the college search and application processes. Overwhelmingly, school counselors are influential and encouraging advocates for students and their aspirations. However, there are some who do not properly research and gauge the college landscape for how it affects Black students. In her memoir *Becoming*, Michelle Obama reflects on an unfortunate encounter she had with her school counselor in high school. In her senior year she met with the counselor she had been assigned and was disappointed when the counselor said, "I'm not sure . . . that you're Princeton material." Imagine how damaging this educational professional's swift and dismissive judgment was for a young Michelle. She stated that she blocked out this memory for a long time and admittedly could not recall the age, race, or any physical characteristics of the counselor. The counselor underestimated the future First Lady. Michelle Obama did wind up attending Princeton University and went on to get a law degree from Harvard Law School. Her experience, however, is not uncommon.

Justice Ketanji Brown Jackson, the first Black woman appointed to the US Supreme Court, also has said she had an unsupportive school counselor, who told her that she'd never get into Harvard. She proved that counselor wrong. We mention these accomplished Black women with the hope that your Black child does not have to disprove the same doubt.

This is a classic case of what we call undermatching. Undermatching happens when a school counselor does not believe in the potential of a student to be a competitive applicant and so may discourage the student and their family from applying to selective schools. Ideally, the family and college counselor should work together to determine what type of school and environment is best for the student. In doing this, both the family and the counselor must be open and honest about the student's preparation, maturity, and, yes, the family's finances. This relationship between family and counselor should begin as early as the ninth grade and be nurtured over the course of four years. For the student to have college admissions success—that is, to have choices in where they go to college—the family and the school counselor have to be transparent about abilities, expectations, and ambitions. The adults have to communicate in order to achieve this goal.

The high school counselors we interviewed in our research worked in public or independent schools. Here are the questions we asked them:

1. How did you get into the college counseling profession?
2. What has been your experience counseling Black students and families?
3. Generally speaking, do Black families come to you with the same amount of college information as families of other races?
4. What do you wish more Black parents knew about college counseling?
5. Do you recommend HBCUs to Black families, and how do they react to the recommendation? What schools—HBCUs or PWIs—are most popular and why?

The responses to questions 1 and 2 varied, and question 5 required some discussion. We were alarmed, though, by the consistent responses we got to questions 3 and 4. We heard that Black families too often gather information about colleges in the spring of their child's eleventh grade or, even worse, in the fall of their twelfth grade. This late timing contrasts with other families, who often visit colleges, encourage extracurricular activities, and explore options for standardized test preparation earlier in their child's high school career. Some may want to attribute this difference to resources, but we disagree. We think it's much more about Black parents being too comfortable with what we know and about not acknowledging how college admissions has changed.

One of the biggest challenges in the college admissions process is that too many people want a voice in what the student should do. Yes, advice from friends and family is well intentioned, yet it is often misinformed. Many people who give advice about college admissions are not professionals in the field. Although they may have gone through the college admissions process with their own child, they should not substitute for a school counselor. A school counselor is supposed to be an authority on the process and can help your student build a balanced college list. The counselor should not be avoided and often is the only person that colleges and universities will share information with about a student's application; thus you are better off engaging with the counselor early on to decide if the information they are sharing—rooted in data and statistics—is applicable to you. Independent college advisors may be able to offer alternative perspectives on college lists and make suggestions for essays and application strategies. In a case where your family hires an independent college advisor, you should let your child's school know about it for the purpose of transparency and clear communication.

We know that some of you may be cautious about school counselors and wonder how they work with Black students after hearing a story like Michelle Obama's. We have similar concerns and will address them below. However, we thought it would be valuable for you to know what school counselors think about themselves, their roles, and your Black children. Here are themes that arose in our conversations with public and private school counselors. These are direct quotations.

On college admissions today . . .

"The criteria to get into college [have] changed a lot in the past fifteen to twenty years since many parents graduated, yet many of them come to the process with assumptions about the process that are often dated and not based in fact. This leads to setting unrealistic expectations, which does not help to set the foundation of the college search process."

On the cost of higher education . . .

"Many families don't have open conversations with their children about the finances. Thus, when students are developing their college list, they have no concept of what the family can and cannot afford when it comes time to make a college choice."

On the importance of starting early . . .

"Depending on the type of college the student is looking to apply to, beginning the process junior and senior year is far too late given some of the curriculum requirements. Most counselors think the process should start at the latest in the ninth grade."

On understanding there are multiple pathways to success . . .

Some "parents come to this process thinking that the only majors that students can be successful in are biology, business, engineering, or a couple of other areas, when the reality is many colleges and universities have [lots of] majors. In addition to that, most of the jobs that are being created are not in many of those areas and have yet to be created."

On the college visit . . .

"Most college counselors feel very strongly [opposed to] students committing to a college . . . they have never visited. Thus, visiting colleges, in person or virtually, if possible, is a very important part of the process."

Parents should always ask their school counselor if they are involved with NACAC (National Association of College Admission Counseling). This is an international professional organization composed of college admissions and high school counselors who work hand-in-hand to guide students from secondary to postsecondary education. All college admissions and college counseling professionals are welcome to join the organization, which provides opportunities for professional development, continuing education, and networking. Given that it costs to be a member and to attend many of the organization's events, NACAC has several initiatives aimed at getting more high school counselors involved in the organization.

Most independent schools have an office dedicated to college counseling with staff members whose sole purpose is to help students with the college admissions process. This office operates independently of the school's counseling office, which handles students' mental health and other counseling needs. Depending on the size of the school, caseloads for counselors could be anywhere between thirty and fifty students per grade. By contrast, many public school counselors have responsibilities beyond college counseling and have caseloads numbering from two hundred to four hundred students or more. One veteran college counselor we interviewed, who had worked at both a large public school and an independent school, had this to say:

"When I was at my independent school, we had thirty juniors and thirty seniors that were in my caseload. When we transitioned to public school, we had a caseload of five hundred students between

the junior and senior classes, where there was no real college-going culture. In addition to the bigger caseloads, there is a belief that the work of counselors does not extend beyond the building; thus your focus should be on the work that needs to happen in the high school and not relationship building with colleges and universities, a luxury we had when I was in the independent school."

Most counselors have a bachelor's degree at a minimum, but many have a master's degree in some form of counseling or in education. There is no such thing, however, as a "college counseling bachelor's degree." While there is a growing number of graduate programs with a college counseling focus, most of them emphasize the guidance and counseling aspect of the job and give little attention to the scope of colleges and universities in the country and around the world. The reality is that most high school and college counselors have to educate themselves about the many colleges and universities available to students.

There are more than four thousand colleges and universities in the United States. It is unrealistic to expect that anyone would know about all of them, but we hope that counselors have a good sense of the different school types that are available. These range from two-year colleges, HBCUs, state schools, and private schools. The guidance that counselors give depends on their knowledge of schools, and if that knowledge is limited, so too will be the suggestions they make to students. In our interviews with school counselors, both Black and white, almost all admitted to having extremely limited understanding of HBCUs beyond the Black Ivies, and those who did understand more tended to be from the South.

This knowledge base is important for Black families who have questions about more than admissions chances, academic majors, and location. They may have questions about resources specific to Black students, the percentage of Black students on campus, graduation and retention rates, and campus climate—questions that may not be as important for their non-Black counterparts. You may have a lot of trust in the college counseling office, but know that you should communicate your child's needs up front to your counselor.

Building a College List

As a college counselor for the past twenty years, I (Shereem) have talked to many students and parents about "match" and "fit." I often urge students to consider who they are, what they want to do, and whether and how a school will help them get there. Students need to understand the importance of finding a school that is right for them, one where they will excel academically and socially and have a college community that suits their personality. Given all the colleges and universities in the United States, I am confident that many schools will match what a student wants. Students or parents who believe that one particular school is the only place where the student will be happy wind up limiting themselves. Researching and visiting colleges can be incredibly fun. Learning about academic programs and extracurricular offerings at colleges can help students find their niche and, ultimately, a career.

One caution: college rankings can serve a valuable purpose, but no one should ever rely on one source to determine what schools are good or not so good. We believe that rankings—*U.S. News and World Report*, *Forbes*, *Princeton Review*—generate interest in schools. They are points of comparison regarding resources, reputation, and facilities. However, there are other factors that students should consider in their decision-making. They need to think about what's important to them—majors, activities, the types of students they want to be with—and how they will make the most of their college years.

My (Shereem's) company offers a service called the College List Builder, which, in essence, is me and my team building a college list for a student. Once I have gathered information from parents and student, I'm able to suggest twenty-plus colleges, given what I know from having visited more than five hundred colleges and universities over the years and from some expensive, exclusive tools that we use. These are not simple algorithms available from free websites; I conduct a data-rich analysis that I use to confirm or reject my initial ideas. We love building lists for families and opening their eyes to schools they may have never heard of or strategies for admission they may have never considered. I build college lists based on four primary factors: *cost, location, possible major,* and *possible career.* Each factor has a distinct importance to the college search process.

Cost

College is very, very expensive. Many of us, including me, are first-generation college students whose parents were blue-collar workers. Having families with limited income and assets, many of us were awarded financial aid packages that were loan-heavy. We know not to let our children take on an exorbitant amount of loan debt. Moreover, if we now have a higher income than our parents had, our children will not qualify for as much financial aid as we did. You and your child must therefore decide how much you are willing to spend or can afford. We are not in favor of taking out excessive college loans. In the chapter "Show Me the Money," we explained some basic elements of financing college and described what you can do to tackle the cost of college.

Location

Where a school is located is something to consider. Is the school in an urban, suburban, or rural setting? What is the weather there like? Many of the most selective schools, as deemed by *U.S. News and World Report,* are in the Northeast, but students who are not from that part of the country should take weather into consideration. Additionally, given that a student will spend four years at a school, they should look into the social and cultural outlets available off campus. Can they mature as a young adult in this environment? Can they get a part-time job off campus if desired? What internship opportunities are available locally? Do the internships often lead to full-time job offers?

Possible Major

Students' primary goal in going to college should be to immerse themselves in an academic field of study that suits their strengths and interests. Their major should be a "practical" one that leads to a career that is both fulfilling and worthy of the financial investment of going to college. Students should have a major in mind when they apply to college. Their choice of major may change, of course, and a liberal arts school encourages students to explore their intellectual interests. Being "undecided" when enrolling in college, however, is often a recipe for wasting time and money. We go into depth about this in chapter 4, "What Is a Liberal Arts Education, and Is It Worth It?" There are personality and career assessment tools that can introduce students to possible majors as early as the tenth grade. Please note, though, we are not advocating that students declare a major in premed, engineering, computer science, or business if they do not have the ambition, high school courses, interest, or strengths to excel in one of these fields. Majors do not equal a career; they just put students on a *possible* (operative word) career path.

Possible Career

We do not know any Black parents who want their child to go to college and come out unemployed or without a plan for having a fulfilling and remunerative career. We want our children to be financially independent and expect college to be the first step toward accomplishing this. A possible major and a possible career go hand-in-hand when building a college list. Having a vision for your child's professional life is not "controlling" them. It's helping them explore options that you know are possible and they may not be aware of. Our duty as parents is to steer our children to their strengths and lead them to majors and careers.

Investigating a college's career guidance office is a must:

- What kinds of career advising happen there?
- What companies does the school have a relationship with?

- How strong is the alumni network?
- What do most alumni do for work soon after graduation, and how much do they earn?

The answer to some of these questions, especially about income after graduation, can be found at the College Scorecard website of the US Department of Education (collegescorecard.ed.gov).

Visiting Colleges: How, Why, and When

Prior to the COVID-19 pandemic, any college admissions officer or college counselor would likely have told you that the best way to find out if a college is right for your child is to visit its campus. With the arrival of the pandemic, however, higher education had to suspend or limit in-person tours, information sessions, and campus programming in favor of giving students and families a virtual semblance of visiting campus. Institutions launched all kinds of virtual platforms to connect with students; the reality, though, is that there is no substitute for visiting a campus in person.

Being able to walk around a campus, drop in at the dining hall, and imagine having a perfect day hanging out on campus helps students find a sense of place at a school. This is something we have witnessed many times: a student visits a campus recommended to them, with no expectations to like it, and by the end of the visit, something has happened that changes the student's mind. The thing is that you never really know what that something will be. It could be a connection with a tour guide, a sunny day on the quadrangle, or a great meal in the dining hall. More often than not, though, it's a general feeling not connected to any one thing about the experience. This feeling usually happens during or shortly after a college visit.

When you begin your college exploration, ideally in your sophomore and junior years of high school, here are our suggestions for how to get a good feel for a school when you visit its campus:

Attend a virtual or in-person (based on availability) information session and go on a tour. While information sessions can sometimes be a bit boring, they are a good way of learning what a school prioritizes. Use this opportunity to learn what the school presents, values, and emphasizes. This will give you insight into what your experience would be like were you to enroll there. Pay attention to the questions asked by other prospective students as well as their cultural and racial backgrounds.

Ask questions. Make sure to ask questions that are important to you and your college exploration process. We suggest having questions prepared prior to attending the information session. Being on campus is your time to find out the things you want to know. Don't leave campus with unanswered questions. There is no question about the academic programs, application review process, or campus culture that you should not be able to get an answer to. Why visit a campus if you are not going to get all the information you need to have an informed opinion about it? (Parents should do the same.)

Speak to a student whom you identify with or share an interest with. You don't have to speak with a Black student, but we do recommend that you speak with someone who has a similar academic interest, is from your hometown, or has another connection with you that matters. While your experience of the school will not be the same as theirs, they can provide you with insight into the campus culture and student experience.

Eat a meal on campus. This is important to do. You should know what dining options are available at the school. No matter how good the food is, you will grow tired of it if you eat it often enough. However, if you don't like the food or the school doesn't have the dietary options you desire, you will know the school's limitations.

Explore on your own. You may not see all that you were wanting to see while on the campus tour. We would advise you to build in some time just to walk around campus and explore areas that you may be interested in. We know that students and families sometimes have the best experiences and conversations on a campus outside the formal tour.

When to Visit

If you want to get the most out of your visit, and we know that you do, you should visit when classes are in session. That is when you can see what the campus "looks" and "feels" like when all the students, faculty, and staff are there. There will be more people around for you to engage with. You will not be limited to what the admissions office or visitor center has to offer. When classes are in session, all the dining halls and student support offices will be open to your exploration.

The ideal time periods for a campus visit are after Labor Day through early November and from late January through April. Depending on the school, there may be limited opportunities to visit in April, given the occurrence of "yield" events related to admitted student programming. Visiting campuses during the summer may be convenient but is not ideal on account of the limited number of students on campus. A few campuses are lively year-round, but they are exceptions to the norm. We know that the months we recommend for visiting campuses are times when high school classes are also in session, but many high schools offer students some excused absences in their senior year for the purpose of visiting colleges.

Demonstrating Interest Can Help
Your Child Get into College

In addition to visiting colleges, we are big advocates of demonstrating interest appropriately. Demonstrating interest is when a prospective student makes documented contact or connections with an institution. Some admissions offices will take this effort into consideration once a student applies for admission. Be sure to ask the schools you are interested in if they track demonstrated interest. Colleges love to be loved. They crave attention from the *right* students at the *right* time. Demonstrating interest to your top-choice schools can be critical to admission. Schools want to know that if they admit a student, there is a good likelihood that the student will enroll. We do not recommend, however, being too aggressive in demonstrating one's interest (assertive = good; aggressive = bad). Here are a few things high school students can do to engage with colleges.

"Like" a school's social media accounts. This is not as trivial as you might think. Colleges track their social media accounts just like most people and businesses do. If a student does not take the time to pop up on a list, do they really want to go there? Like a school on Facebook and follow it on Twitter and Instagram. Make sure to mention your top-choice schools in your own posts and tweets. And say nice things.

Have an interview. If a school offers interviews, then get some quality face-time with a student ambassador, alumni interviewer, or an admissions officer. Many private colleges (and some public ones) offer prospective students the opportunity for an interview before they apply or afterward. These interviews help a student learn more about the college and help the college learn more about the student. Check the admissions office's website for this opportunity.

Write amazing supplemental essays. Nothing screams "I love you; please take me!" louder than knockout school-specific supplemental essays. In them, students can explain why they are a perfect fit for a school. In their applications, many colleges will ask directly, "Why do you want to come here?" Others will ask questions that reference their school's mission or strengths. The purpose of these essays is to gauge how much the student knows about the school and how well they will fit in at the school. Be sure to use your own voice and not just regurgitate what's on the school's website. Admissions officers like me (Tim) see right through this, so it is important to be original. Doing research about the school and demonstrating personal pizazz are key to good supplemental essays.

Early Decision and Early Action are *huge* indicators of sincere interest. Applying Early Decision is the strongest way to show a college that it is your number-one choice. This is why most colleges accept Early Decision applicants at a much higher rate than regular decision applicants. Early Decision is not for everyone, though, so if you aren't ready to commit to one school early in the game, apply Early Action instead, which still shows a high level of interest. It is important to submit applications before the deluge of other applicants submit theirs.

College Events to Attend

There are times of the school year when you can get a better feel for a campus than others; likewise there are events you can attend that can create a special connection and experience. While these experiences can provide you a glimpse into what your college experience could be, they will not reflect the totality of the college experience you will have. These events include going to a college rivalry game, such as Duke versus the University of North Carolina in college basketball, or being in the stands for the Bayou Classic football game in New Orleans between Grambling State University and Southern University.

Southern University and A&M College (HBCU)
Baton Rouge, LA
6,200 Undergraduates
Public
Graduate Students: Yes
Setting: Midsize City

These events can truly be exciting, and, yes, they are a part of the college experience for many. But think about the college experience outside these special events. What will your experience be like then? We are not trying to deter anyone from enjoying such events; rather, we are encouraging students and families to think about the daily experience that students will have at that institution. Many who attend college will have memories of going to the "big game," but more than that, they will remember the friends they met in the residence hall, the professor who pushed them in class, and the lessons they learned that stuck with them after graduation.

HBCU Homecomings

If you visit an HBCU on an ordinary day, you may not be impressed with the campus grounds as you would be at a well-endowed PWI. To truly get a feel for these schools and what they can offer you in your college experience, we suggest that you visit on homecoming weekend. At homecoming, the campus really comes alive, and you can see what the school can provide students in identity and culture apart from what the school may seem to lack in resources. Homecoming at an HBCU is the epitome of the Black college experience. You will experience the essence of the school—its students, alumni, and rich history and culture. An HBCU homecoming is one of the greatest testaments to Black love, Black education, and Black accomplishment, and we encourage all to take part in one at least once.

Admissions Tests: ACT or SAT?

Standardized testing and standardized test preparation are both complicated. They are lucrative businesses and have become fixtures in college admissions. Many of the more selective schools in the United States require testing in some form for admissions. Testing has its benefits. It also has its drawbacks. The merits of standardized testing have been debated for decades, but COVID-19 disrupted higher education in ways that have pushed this debate further. While there was a growing number of schools that had test-optional admissions before the pandemic, COVID-19 pushed schools to offer test-optional admissions on account of the uncertainty about public health safety at testing sites. According to FairTest.org, in 2021 over 75 percent of US colleges and universities offering bachelor's degrees were either test-optional or test-blind, an all-time high. We think this is a trend that will continue for the foreseeable future, but many of these schools have not made a long-term commitment to being test-optional beyond the next few years. In addition to many institutions going test-optional, the NCAA will not require students to take a standardized test to meet the NCAA's initial eligibility requirements for Division I or II athletics through the 2022–23 academic year. Despite these suspended requirements, testing is still part of the fabric of college admissions.

We encourage families to examine how standardized tests are used and how to make testing benefit their student in the admissions process. We encourage all Black parents to consider investing in standardized test prep for their child because test scores are valuable information for many institutions. When your child scores well on the ACT or SAT, your child will be viewed as more competitive, and a good score may increase their chances of qualifying for scholarship money.

Standardized test scores are numbers that most admissions offices have depended on in evaluating applicants for a long time. Grades can be inflated, and curricula vary from high school to high school. Some schools have International Baccalaureate programs and others have Advanced Placement courses. Some schools have neither, so it's hard for colleges' admissions offices to evaluate students who had different course offerings or grading systems. The SAT and ACT, on the other hand, are common denominators that can give colleges a basis for comparing one student with another. Traditionally, these tests are viewed as measuring "aptitude." That may be a flawed way of thinking about them, but that's how admissions offices at some schools operate. When students are asked by friends or family about college, they are often asked "What are your test scores?" and "What is your GPA?" Seldom are they asked about their activities, recommendations, essays, or interviews.

Having a higher score on a test will open more doors. We also understand, however, that there are good test takers and those who don't test well. How well a student performs on standardized tests should determine if test-optional admission is the better choice.

Although taking standardized tests and buying stocks on the market are different things, I (Tim) found an analogy between them in a stock tip related to me by a friend. This friend, who works for an investment bank, was suggesting some possible stocks to invest in amid the pandemic. As he shared with me several options, some of them being tech plays, others being higher risk in the retail market, he ended by saying, "you can't go wrong with oil." He explained that while oil was currently down owing to low demand, there will continue to be a need for oil in future generations, even with our increased exploration and use of alternative energy sources. He concluded that oil will probably be around at least through our grandchildren's lives.

In the world of college admissions, testing is oil; it is not going anywhere anytime soon. Yes, some schools have become test-optional, and the pandemic increased the number of schools offering that option, but many of those schools may offer test-optional admissions only until things get back to normal. Then they will reinstate the requirement of testing in their admissions review.

Students and families may wonder if they should take the tests and submit scores with their applications. There is no one right answer to this question; the truth is that you should do what is best for your student based on the schools they are looking to apply to. With so many variables in the college application process, no one factor is determinant, but testing is near the top of the list.

We think that many of those who are reading this book understand the *why* of applying to college, but just as important is the *how*. In this chapter we gave an overview of important parts in the admissions process to help ensure student success. As we were writing, we came across an article that quantified the information disparity that exists between Black families and white families when it comes to assisting students with the college admissions process.

Susan Adams, in a December 2021 article in *Forbes* titled "White Students Have an Advantage in College Admissions," reported the results of a survey in which more than two-thirds of white students said they relied on family and friends to help them with college admissions, whereas only 38 percent of Black students got similar advice from their families. It is our goal through this book to close this gap so that Black families are better able to assist their children through the process of college admissions.

Acknowledgments

Tim

To my SpelHouse family: there are too many of you to name. But for all of those who allowed me to pick your brains, shared your family experiences to help me craft this book, have been down with me over the past twenty-five years, and continue to inspire me with all the great things you do, know that it means the world to me. Attending college in the Atlanta University Center is one of the best decisions I made in life and continues to be a great source of inspiration because of all of you.

This book would never have been possible without the support of Emory University. Over my past twenty years, this great institution has allowed me to find my passion in an environment that aspires to be more than simply a place to go to college; rather, it aspires to be a destination where students transform their lives through sharing knowledge and creating community. All the wonderful, talented, and inspiring colleagues I have had the honor of working with, please know that each of you has made an impact on me and that this work would not have been possible without your reassurance. I often say that I have not worked a day since I arrived, and that is all because of you. To John Latting and Scott Allen, thank you for letting me be me; there is no way this book could exist without your support and encouragement.

To my Gates Millennium Scholars, UNCF, National Merit, QuestBridge, TRiO, and TDI families, along with all of the great admissions professionals and community-based organizations I have had the opportunity to work with from both sides of the desk—I can't thank you enough for being such a great source of inspiration and for the knowledge you have shared on top of all the great things you do to impact the lives of students looking to access higher education and beyond.

Shereem, thank you for picking up the phone to call me and then believing enough in me to let me take this journey with you.

You may not have wanted me to answer your call, but I did, and your passion for this topic remains the catalyst for this important conversation. To my mother, father, sister, and brother, not a day goes by that I am not thankful for your presence in my life. Each of you has believed in me from day one, and I love you so much for it. This does not happen without the trips down I-20 from Dallas to Waskom and the foundation you all continue to provide me. And to all my day 1's from Texas, you "already" know!

Finally, Master Alexander, Miss Carter, Skinny, TT, and my rock Britney—thank you for the daily hugs, laughs, and inspiration. None of this happens without all the support you have given me throughout this process as I was locked in my lair writing.

Shereem

The historian Herman Dreer was a teacher, writer, author, and lecturer. I need to acknowledge how his writing on the brotherhood of Negro college men inspires me to do my best to be all that he was.

This book is a product of Tim's and my commitment to service. It's important that we start there. Everyone else who contributed to this book in some capacity did so because they too wanted to serve others. We appreciate the time and effort of all the people we spoke to about this project because you gave us insight and fuel.

To Greg Britton—thank you and your team at Johns Hopkins University Press for being excited and supportive from the beginning. You believe in us and we appreciate it.

To Brennan Barnard, Rick Clark, and Jeff Selingo—you guys set the table for us and shared your resources. Thank you.

To Cathleen Trigg-Jones and Dr. Tony Allen, president of Delaware State University—more than you know, you inspired our work and confirmed that it was important and necessary.

To some of the best people I know from Brooklyn Friends, Westtown, Wesleyan, Breadloaf, and work life: André Wright, Ross Stafford, Shawn Marshall, Stephen Valentine, Anthony Ross, Kapr Bangura, Donald Bull, Chris Richardson, Aaron Howard, Sharif

Williams, Demetrius Montrose, Marie Bigham, Tamar Adegbile, Kwesi Fraser, André Pinard, Nakia Booth, Kim Cooper, Dan Limerick, Duke Amponsah, Susan Tree, Peter Snedecor, Rhonda and Gary Casson, Patty and Michael Chernick, Jill and Paul Aschkenasy, and Dianne Garrett.

For those whose words poured into me then and keep me going now: Gail Karpf, Marysol Castro, Darrick Hamilton, Monique Nelson-Nwachuku, Auntie Irene, Anaya, Primo Khalil, and Mom and Dad. I truly do love you.

And to Tim. You used to say "no new friends," and my feelings were hurt. Not anymore. You have been the rock of this project, and I thank you for all that you have brought to the work and to my life. We share a love of Black people and want them to have the information to soar. Thank you for allowing me to be the Robin (or Alfred?) to your Batman. (But I'm 3000!)

In Our Opinion

Shereem

College is not for everyone. Despite what I do for a living and how I am raising my own children, I am not 100 percent convinced that every Black child should go to college, especially not an expensive one that may put them in debt.

From my personal experience as a parent, I am learning that students see college more as an opportunity to have a "good time" than as an educational springboard to adulthood. While this troubles me at times, I am not sure that I viewed college any differently as a teenager. When you're young, you believe you'll always be young, and if you plan on going to college, you may not think about life too far after it. We should encourage our children to have a plan for their lives at age twenty-two and beyond. Because college is such a short window of time in our lives, it should not be the primary destination on the journey of a life well lived.

No matter when we declare ourselves to be an adult, most of us begin learning what we want to learn and how we want to learn it when we're ready. The internet has changed how we educate ourselves, and traditional college may not be right for everyone, although I agree that socializing is not the same without the microcosm of a college campus. We, as parents, should help our children decide what's really important for the marathon of life.

If you want your child to go to college and your child wants to go to college, I want what you want. If you do not want your child to go to college and they do not either, I will not judge you or them, but I will ask you, What's the plan? College gives us the structure and boundaries to formulate a vision for the future. There are resources there that help young people find themselves and get their professional footing. If going to college is what your family has decided to do, you need to educate yourselves on the college options out there and be proactive in finding the right places to visit and ultimately help your child to apply.

College admissions at elite schools—HBCUs and PWIs—can be complicated. Many of us overlook schools that might serve our child better because we believe that a name and a network are critical to success in life. In my opinion, this is true, so if your child is going to go to college, they should have in mind schools with a name and network that will excite them to be on campus and thrive. If, however, your child is an artist, an athlete, or someone intent on finding their own way to success, I hope we can get behind them and applaud their courage. Might they ultimately regret the decision not to attend college? Maybe. Do we all know people we respect and applaud who do not have a college degree? Likely so. The choice is not just between an HBCU and a PWI; the question is, Is college right for my child?

Tim

Throughout this book our goal has been to offer a fair and balanced view on the benefits of both PWIs and HBCUs, but everyone wants to know what we really think. We must have a preference, right? No, we don't, but we have so many opinions. If you had asked me this question—about PWIs versus HBCUs—fifteen to twenty years ago, I would have told you that every Black student, especially Black males, should attend an HBCU, but my personal and professional opinion has evolved over time. For starters, it is not realistic. While there are over a hundred HBCUs across the country, there is simply not enough room at these fine institutions to educate all the Black students who want to go to college. More importantly, Black people are not and have never been monolithic, so the notion that Black students would only want to attend HBCUs does not reflect the reality of all Black families' educational aspirations. If the desire behind wanting all Black students to attend HBCUs is to shield them from this country's racist ills, that is naïve as well. The reality is that Black students need options for their college education, and they need schools that will provide them with the support, resources, and education they need to thrive while in school and succeed in their professional lives.

The decision to go to college is a personal one, and students will be drawn to different things in their college search. The prestige of institutions will drive some, others will lean toward athletic power-houses, and some will be drawn to HBCUs for social and cultural reasons; but the reality is that most will choose a school based on finances, proximity to their family, or other personal circumstances unrelated to the school. Knowing this from my professional experience, I don't prefer HBCUs over PWIs categorically; what I advise, rather, is finding a school that will meet the needs of the family and the student. We all say that it's the student's decision, but the reality is that it's a family decision, and there are any number of circumstances that can influence the choice of a college. I can offer an opinion, of course, but the truth is that I don't know your child, your family, or your situation.

I would love it if every Black male attended Morehouse, but do they want to be in Atlanta? Do they want to attend an all-male school? Does Morehouse have the academic programs they are looking for? And will the school offer the financial aid they need? Is Emory a great institution? Yes. It has been my professional home for the better part of twenty years. But Emory is selective, is a Division III athletic school with no football team, and may not have the diversity a student or family is looking for. I could continue with any number of institutions, and there will be just as many questions given the personal nature of college choice.

What I want is for your family to be candid and open in the college admissions process from beginning to end. If money is a determining factor, explain that to your child up front because that will limit the schools you consider in the college search. If proximity is a priority, factor that in as early as possible. If HBCUs are not an option, ask yourself why. We can talk about the pros and cons of HBCUs versus PWIs. What we can't do, though, is speak to your child's needs, determine what you can afford, or know what is most important to your family in this process.

I do have one very strong opinion about the college admissions process: it should be based on information, and you should make decisions within the walls of your home and not be influenced by those who don't know all that goes into your making this important life decision. If you and your family own this process early, I have no doubt that your child will have an incredible experience at whatever institution your family chooses.

Best Colleges for Black Students

Parents are always asking us, Where should my child apply? We love this question because it allows us to ask about a student's interests, strengths, and aspirations.

Building a college list does not happen in a three-minute conversation off the top of our heads, but we have become familiar with many colleges and universities that we admire and recommend that parents and students research.

Below is a list of schools, by states, that we recommend to families. We mentioned many of them in the book already. We have also included some additional names. Please note that there are many other great schools for Black students we didn't list, but we wanted to provide a starting point for families based on our experiences, feedback from families and college counselors, and other factors such as cost, location, majors, and career exploration opportunities.

New York/New Jersey
Barnard College (women's college)
Binghamton University
Colgate University
Columbia University
Cornell University
Fordham University
Hamilton College
New York University
Princeton University
Rochester Institute of Technology
Rutgers University
Sarah Lawrence College
Syracuse University

University of Rochester
Vassar College

Connecticut/Rhode Island
Brown University
Connecticut College
Trinity College
University of Connecticut
Wesleyan University
Yale University

Massachusetts/New Hampshire/Vermont/Maine
Amherst College
Bates College
Boston College
Boston University
Bowdoin College
Dartmouth College
Harvard University
Massachusetts Institute of Technology
Middlebury College
Mount Holyoke College (women's college)
Northeastern University
Smith College (women's college)
Tufts University
University of Massachusetts at Amherst
Wellesley College (women's college)
Williams College

Pennsylvania
Bryn Mawr College (women's college)
Bucknell University
Carnegie Mellon

Dickinson College
Drexel University
Haverford College
Lehigh University
Swarthmore College
Temple University
University of Pennsylvania
Villanova University

HBCUs
Cheyney University of Pennsylvania
Lincoln University

Delaware/District of Columbia/Maryland/Virginia

American University
College of William and Mary
Georgetown University
George Washington University
James Madison University
Johns Hopkins University
Towson University
Trinity Washington University
University of Maryland–College Park
University of Richmond
University of Virginia

HBCUs
Bowie State University
Delaware State University
Hampton University
Howard University
Morgan State University
Norfolk State University
Virginia State University
Virginia Union University

North Carolina / South Carolina

Clemson University
Davidson College
Duke University
Elon University
University of North Carolina–Chapel Hill
Wake Forest University

HBCUs

Elizabeth City State University
Johnson C. Smith University
North Carolina A&T State University
North Carolina Central University
Shaw University
South Carolina State University
Winston-Salem State University

Georgia / Florida / Tennessee

Agnes Scott College (women's college)
Emory University
Florida State University
Georgia State University
Georgia Tech University
University of Florida
University of Georgia
University of Miami
University of Tennessee–Knoxville
Vanderbilt University

HBCUs

Clark Atlanta University
Fisk University
Florida A&M University
Fort Valley State University

Morehouse College (men's college)
Savannah State University
Spelman College (women's college)
Tennessee State University

Alabama / Mississippi / Louisiana
Tulane University

HBCUs
Alabama State University
Alcorn State University
Dillard University
Grambling State University
Jackson State University
Southern University and A&M College
Talladega College
Tuskegee University
Xavier University of Louisiana

Arkansas / Oklahoma / Texas
Rice University
Southern Methodist University
Texas Christian University
University of Houston
University of Oklahoma
University of Texas–Arlington
University of Texas–Austin

HBCUs
Langston University
Paul Quinn College
Philander Smith College
Prairie View A&M University
Texas Southern University

University of Arkansas–Pine Bluff
Wiley College

Illinois / Kentucky / Michigan / Ohio / Indiana / Missouri
Berea College
Case Western University
Kenyon College
Northwestern University
Notre Dame University
Oberlin College
University of Chicago
University of Michigan
University of Missouri–Columbia
Washington University in St. Louis

HBCUs
Central State University
Wilberforce University

California / Colorado
California Institute of Technology
Claremont McKenna College
Colorado College
Harvey Mudd College
Occidental College
Pomona College
Scripps College (women's college)
Stanford University
University of California–Berkeley
University of California–Los Angeles
University of Denver
University of Southern California

Frequently Asked Questions

College Search

What standardized tests should my child take and when?
This is a personal decision, but we would encourage families to explore free test preparation through books or online resources. Students can take a diagnostic test for both the SAT and ACT to see which one would be better to take. Others would encourage students to take both tests to see which one they do better on, and then focus on taking that test again. There is no wrong answer here; it really depends on what the student is most comfortable with. Ideally, they should not take either test more than three times.

When should test preparation begin?
We recommend starting test prep in the summer after tenth grade. Preparing for the ACT or SAT is not about cramming. Preparation should be gradual because it takes time to learn test-taking strategies and to practice them. Ideally, if a student decides to test, they should have a score they are comfortable with by the beginning of their senior year.

What activities should students do while in high school?
Unless a school asks for specific activities, and most do not, schools simply want to know that a student is authentically interested and productive in an activity outside the classroom. If anything, schools are looking for consistency and commitment to a student's chosen areas of interest.

What if my child has learning differences?
The short answer is **there are no IEPs (Individualized Education Programs) or 504 plans in college.** The Individuals with Disabilities Education Act, the law that provides students with IEPs, no longer applies to them once they graduate from high school. Thus,

it's important to contact schools prior to applying to learn about services and accommodations they offer for students with learning differences.

When should we start visiting colleges?

As early as a student's eighth or ninth grade, a family should visit schools any chance they get when they go to see extended family or friends who live near schools of interest. We believe that students should earnestly begin visiting schools as early as the summer following their sophomore year of high school.

Should we be taking virtual tours?

While it's always better to visit a campus in person to get a feel for its culture, the pandemic has pushed schools to increase virtual touring opportunities. Our advice is to try to visit the schools you are most interested in, and for others you may be on the fence about, look into virtual tours.

What should we do when representatives of a college visit our school or area?

Visiting all your schools of interest may be difficult to do. If representatives of a school of interest come to town for a prospective student program, then we encourage the family or student to attend. If the family has already visited that school or taken part in another of its programs, there is no need to attend again, unless the school tracks demonstrated interest.

What is dual enrollment? Should we consider it?

Dual enrollment is when college courses are offered to high school students while they are still in high school. The transfer of these course credits varies by institution, so it's good to have an idea of the schools a student plans to apply to before deciding to take part in dual enrollment. Dual enrollment credits are more likely to transfer to in-state public colleges and universities. If a student wants to apply to some of the more selective schools in the country, they should considerer enrolling in Advanced Placement or

International Baccalaureate courses offered at their high school, if they are available, as opposed to enrolling in dual enrollment. What's most important in thinking about dual enrollment is considering whether the courses will be accepted for credit by the institutions the student applies to. Thus, before enrolling in dual enrollment courses, we recommend that the family contact schools of interest and ask them if they accept dual enrollment credits and what is the maximum number of credits an incoming first-year student can bring in. Many private colleges and universities limit the number of dual enrollment credits they accept from those who enroll as first-year students.

Do colleges look at students' social media posts? What kinds of posts are inappropriate?
Students need to know that social media can be used for them or against them. Too often students believe their digital imprint is "private" without realizing that it isn't necessarily. We recommend that students use social media to support their applications, not as public displays meant only for their friends. If a high school student wants to use social media, we would discourage them from posting anything they are not willing to share with the schools they're considering.

College Applications

What is needed for a college application?
The requirements for a college application vary from school to school. Most schools, though, will require the following:
- application form
- essay(s)
- transcript
- tests scores (ACT, SAT, or Advanced Placement scores if applicable; currently many schools are test-optional, so check with individual schools for testing requirements)
- teacher recommendations
- counselor recommendation, or School Report Form

We advise families to visit a school's admissions website to learn about its particular requirements.

How many colleges should my student apply to?
While there is no one-size-fits-all answer, we encourage students to have a balanced college list that includes

- reach schools—those where a student has less than a 25 percent chance of being admitted;
- target schools—those where a student has a 50 percent chance of being admitted; and
- foundational schools—those where a student has a 75 percent chance or better of being admitted.

We think that having three of each (nine schools in total) is a good strategy. *The percentages are based on schools' published admit rates; schools publish ranges for the academic credentials of their last admitted class, and students can compare those ranges with their own credentials to estimate a likelihood of their being admitted.*

What should the college application essay be about?
The college application essay, also known as the personal statement, needs to be honest and revealing. There is no one thing it should be about. Essays should respond to prompts, and leave the reader with takeaways about who the applicant is.

What are supplemental essays? Why are they important?
Supplemental essays are pieces of writing, ranging from 150 words to 650 words, that a school may ask for in addition to the personal statement. The purpose of supplemental essays is usually to see how a candidate thinks, while the personal statement is intended to reveal part of who the candidate is. Supplemental essays are important, oftentimes especially so for smaller college communities.

What are colleges looking for in recommendations? Who should write them?
Recommendation letters are a way for schools to find out additional information about students, specifically related to their intellectual

curiosity and character in the classroom. They provide insight into the type of student an applicant would be in college. Given that there's much weight placed on students' academic potential in admissions decisions, teachers are often the best recommender for giving insight into their students' abilities because of the large amount of time they spend with their students. A family can contact a school to find out what categories of recommenders it accepts recommendations from.

When are applications due?

Most schools begin accepting applications on August 1. However, the final deadline is usually October 15, November 1, November 15, December 1, or January 1. Each institution sets its own deadlines, so they will vary. All students should aim to have their applications submitted in advance of the deadlines.

Are interviews important?

If a college offers an interview—in person, virtual, or with alumni— a student should take advantage of the opportunity. This is a chance for them to ask questions and share who they are and why they are a good match for the school.

What is demonstrated interest?

Demonstrated interest is when institutions consider an applicant's engagement with them during the application process in making their admissions decision. What is considered demonstrated interest varies from school to school, so the best thing to do is ask schools two questions:

(a) Does the school consider demonstrated interest?
(b) What actions count as demonstrated interest?

When should we apply for financial aid?

Each school has its own financial aid deadlines. We recommend that families apply for financial aid in the fall of a student's senior year in high school.

Should we fill out the FAFSA even though we make a lot of money?
Absolutely. How financial aid eligibility is determined varies from
school to school. The worst that can happen is a school will turn
down a family's application for need-based financial aid. To be eligible for merit aid instead, schools usually need to have the FAFSA
and/or CSS Profile on file.

When will we be notified of an admissions decision?
This will depend on what admissions plan an applicant applies
under: Early Action, Single-Choice Early Action, Early Decision I,
Early Decision II, regular decision, or rolling. Students will have
heard from all colleges by early April of their senior year and must
make a decision by May 1, which was designated College Signing
Day by First Lady Michelle Obama.

College Choice

What should we prioritize in choosing a college?
A family should have an honest conversation about what factors
are the most important in determining which college or university
is the best choice. The choice may be driven by cost, location, diversity, possible majors, career aspirations, or any number of other
reasons. We encourage families to have some kind of a system in
place for determining the factors that matter the most.

How do we compare financial aid packages?
Financial aid packages will differ from one institution to the next.
Families should look at all aid packages together and consider the
bottom-line out-of-pocket expense. The out-of-pocket expense may
not be the determining factor in a family's college choice, but we
think it's important to consider it. A great resource for comparing
financial aid packages is the FinAide app, finaideapp.com.

When does the decision about which college to attend have to be made?
This will vary from school to school, but for many schools in the
country, the deadline is May 1. Some schools are willing to grant

an extension to accepted applicants who need more time, but such applicants will need to contact the schools before May 1 to make arrangements.

What happens when a student is waitlisted?

A student who's waitlisted is at the mercy of the school as to when they'll hear the school's decision. Each school has its own waitlist procedure, so it's important for waitlisted students to learn about next steps as soon as they receive the waitlisted notification. Even if that school is the student's top choice, we advise the student to begin thinking about other options.

What is a gap year?

A gap year is when a student does not go to college immediately after graduating from high school. There are studies showing that many students are burnt out after thirteen consecutive years of school and need a year to mature and rejuvenate with a job, travel, or activity. They can then go to college refreshed and ready. We highly recommend that students go ahead and apply to college anyway during their senior year of high school. After being admitted to a college, a student can then pursue the possibility of deferring enrollment for a year.

What is an admissions deposit?

An admissions deposit is usually a nonrefundable deposit that students have to pay to hold their spot in an entering class. The fee varies from school to school, but generally it ranges from one hundred to eight hundred dollars.

Notable Black College Graduates Mentioned in the Book

Person	College/University	Institutional Type	Accomplishments
Kareem Abdul-Jabbar	University of California, Los Angeles	PWI	NBA Player, Author, Actor, Civil Rights Activist
Stacey Abrams	Spelman College	HBCU	Lawyer, Activist, Politician
Byron Allen	University of Southern California	PWI	Comedian, Business Executive
Debbie Allen	Howard University	HBCU	Choreographer, Actor, Producer
Anthony Anderson	Howard University	HBCU	Actor, Producer
Julian Bond	Morehouse College	HBCU	Civil Rights Leader
Chadwick Boseman	Howard University	HBCU	Actor
Rosalind Brewer	Spelman College	HBCU	Business Executive
Herman Cain	Morehouse College	HBCU	Business Executive
Kenneth Chenault	Bowdoin College	PWI	Business Executive
Shirley Chisholm	Brooklyn College	PWI	US Representative, Educator, Author
Jim Clyburn	South Carolina State University	HBCU	US Representative

(continued)

Notable Black College Graduates Mentioned in the Book (*continued*)

Person	College/University	Institutional Type	Accomplishments
Bill Cosby	Temple University	PWI	Actor, Comedian
Morgan DeBaun	Washington University in St. Louis	PWI	Entrepreneur
Thasunda Brown Duckett	University of Houston	PWI	Business Executive
Michael Eric Dyson	Princeton University	PWI	Author, Professor
Kamilah Forbes	Howard University	HBCU	Producer, Filmmaker
Eddie George	Ohio State University	PWI	NFL Player, Head Coach College Football
Amanda Gorman	Harvard College	PWI	National Youth Poet Laureate
Kamala Harris	Howard University	HBCU	US Vice President
Taraji P. Henson	Howard University	HBCU	Actor
Langston Hughes	Lincoln University	HBCU	Poet, Social Activist
Zora Neale Hurston	Howard University	HBCU	Author, Anthropologist, Filmmaker
Terrence J	North Carolina A&T State University	HBCU	Actor, TV Host
Hue Jackson	University of the Pacific	PWI	NFL Coach, Head Coach College Football
Rev. Jesse Jackson Sr.	North Carolina A&T State University	HBCU	Civil Rights Activist, Minister

Person	College/University	Institutional Type	Accomplishments
Samuel L. Jackson	Morehouse College	HBCU	Actor
Robert "Bob" L. Johnson	Princeton University	PWI	Entrepreneur, Media Mogul
Vernon Jordan	Howard University	HBCU	Business Executive, Civil Rights Attorney
Dr. Martin Luther King Jr.	Morehouse College	HBCU	Civil Rights Leader
Mathew Knowles	Fisk University	HBCU	Business Executive
Spike Lee	Morehouse College	HBCU	Film Director
John Lewis	Fisk University	HBCU	US Representative, Civil Rights Leader
Thurgood Marshall	Lincoln University	HBCU	US Supreme Court Justice
Toni Morrison	Howard University	HBCU	Poet, Novelist
Edwin Moses	Morehouse College	HBCU	Olympic Gold Medalist
Barack Obama	Columbia University	PWI	US President
Michelle Obama	Princeton University	PWI	First Lady, Author, Lawyer
Pam Oliver	Florida A&M University	HBCU	Sports Broadcaster
William Packer	Florida A&M University	HBCU	Film Director, Producer

(continued)

Notable Black College Graduates Mentioned in the Book (*continued*)

Person	College/University	Institutional Type	Accomplishments
Dick Parsons	University of Hawai'i at Mānoa	PWI	Business Executive
Megan Jovon Ruth Pete a.k.a. Megan Thee Stallion	Texas Southern University	HBCU	Hip-Hop Artist
Phylicia Rashad	Howard University	HBCU	Actor, Director, Singer
Steven Reed	Morehouse College	HBCU	Mayor
Condoleezza Rice	University of Denver	PWI	US Secretary of State, Professor
Jerry Rice	Mississippi Valley State University	HBCU	NFL Player
Cedric Richmond	Morehouse College	HBCU	US Representative
Shonda Rhimes	Dartmouth College	PWI	Screenwriter, Producer
Eric Roberson	Howard University	HBCU	Singer, Songwriter
Tracee Ellis Ross	Brown University	PWI	Actor, Producer
Deion Sanders	Talladega College (Played college football at Florida State University)	HBCU	NFL Player, TV Personality, Head Coach College Football
Shannon Sharpe	Savannah State University	HBCU	NFL Player, TV Personality

Person	College/University	Institutional Type	Accomplishments
John Singleton	University of Southern California	PWI	Film Director, Screenwriter, Producer, Actor
Robert F. Smith	Cornell University	PWI	Businessman, Philanthropist, Engineer
Stephen A. Smith	Winston-Salem State University	HBCU	Sports Journalist, TV Personality
David Steward	University of Central Missouri	PWI	Business Executive
Michael Strahan	Texas Southern University	HBCU	NFL Player, TV Personality
Beverly Daniel Tatum	Wesleyan University	PWI	Psychologist, Author, Educator
Tristan Walker	State University of New York at Stony Brook	PWI	Entrepreneur
Raphael Warnock	Morehouse College	HBCU	US Senator, Minister
Susan Kelechi Watson	Howard University	HBCU	Actress
Oprah Winfrey	Tennessee State University	HBCU	Media Mogul, Philanthropist
Randall Woodfin	Morehouse College	HBCU	Mayor
Andrew Young	Howard University	HBCU	Mayor, Ambassador, Civil Rights Leader

Suggested Reading

Barnard, Brennan, and Rick Clark. *The Truth about College Admission: A Family Guide to Getting In and Staying Together* (2019).

Bruni, Frank. *Where You Go Is Not Who You'll Be: An Antidote to the College Admissions Mania* (2016).

Cole, J. *Get 'em Out: Help Your Teen Discover a Successful Path to College (. . . and Out of Your House)* (2019).

DiAngelo, Robin. *White Fragility: Why It's So Hard for White People to Talk about Racism* (2018).

Dyson, Michael Eric. *Entertaining Race: Performing Blackness in America* (2021).

Freeman, Kassie. *African Americans and College Choice: The Influence of Family and School* (2005).

Furda, Eric J., and Jacques Steinberg. *The College Conversation: A Practical Companion for Parents to Guide Their Children along the Path to Higher Education* (2020).

Graham, Lawrence Otis. *Our Kind of People: Inside America's Black Upper Class* (1999).

Heffernan, Lisa, and Mary Dell Harrington. *Grown and Flown: How to Support Your Teen, Stay Close as a Family, and Raise Independent Adults* (2019).

Horn, Michael B., and Bob Moesta. *Choosing College: How to Make Better Learning Decisions throughout Your Life* (2019).

Jack, Anthony Abraham. *The Privileged Poor: How Elite Colleges Are Failing Disadvantaged Students* (2019).

Lieber, Ron. *The Price You Pay for College: An Entirely New Road Map for the Biggest Financial Decision Your Family Will Ever Make* (2021).

Marcus, David L. *Acceptance: A Legendary Guidance Counselor Helps Seven Kids Find the Right Colleges—and Find Themselves* (2009).

Mitchell, Josh. *The Debt Trap: How Student Loans Became a National Catastrophe* (2021).

Obama, Michelle. *Becoming* (2018).

ONeal, Anthony. *The Debt Free Degree: The Step-by-Step Guide to Getting Your Kid through College without Student Loans* (2019).

Pope, Loren. *Colleges That Change Lives: 40 Schools That Will Change the Way You Think about Colleges* (2006).

Sabky, Becky Munsterer. *Valedictorians at the Gate: Standing Out, Getting In, and Staying Sane While Applying to College* (2021).

Scott, Carjie. *You Are Accepted: How to Get Accepted into College and Life* (2021).

Selingo, Jeffrey. *Who Gets In and Why: A Year inside College Admissions* (2020).

Tanabe, Gen, and Kelly Tanabe. *The Ultimate Scholarship Book, 2022: Billions of Dollars in Scholarships, Grants and Prizes* (2021).

Tatum, Beverly Daniel. *Why Are All the Black Kids Sitting Together in the Cafeteria? And Other Conversations about Race* (1997).

Tough, Paul. *The Years That Matter Most: How College Makes or Breaks Us* (2019).

Walker, Sheryl. *The Black Girl's Guide to College Success: What No One Really Tells You about College That You Must Know* (2007).

Wilkerson, Isabel. *Caste: The Origins of Our Discontents* (2020).

Zasloff, Beth, and Joshua Steckel. *Hold Fast to Dreams: A College Guidance Counselor, His Students, and the Vision of a Life beyond Poverty* (2015).

Glossary

accreditation. The recognition by an outside agency that a school maintains certain curricular standards. Having a degree from an accredited institution lets students qualify for admission to other accredited institutions.

ACT (American College Test). A standardized test that is often required for admission to college. The test is divided into four sections: English, Math, Reading, and Science.

admissions requirements. A set of rules established by every college or university for determining whether students qualify for admission.

Advanced Placement (AP). Advanced high school classes that allow students to earn credit that can be transferred to a college and may let them bypass entry-level college courses. Credit is earned only if a student earns a high enough score on a standardized test. Most highly selective schools expect applicants to have taken AP courses in high school.

AP Scholar. An award recognizing high school students who have shown college-level achievement through their performance on multiple AP tests. There are several levels to the award.

associate's degree. An associate's degree is earned after completing a program of study at a two-year college, typically a community or junior college. The degree is usually an associate of arts or an associate of science.

audit. When a student attends a class for the purpose of gaining information without completing all assignments or taking all tests. No grade or credit is given.

bachelor's degree. A degree awarded for completing a college academic program of at least four years. These degrees are usually a bachelor of arts (BA) or a bachelor of science (BS).

CEEB Code (College Entrance Examination Board Code). A unique identification number assigned to each high school and college. This code appears on the high school profile or can be obtained from a school counselor or searched for online.

College Board. A nonprofit organization that provides tests and other educational services for students, high schools, and colleges. The SAT (Scholastic Assessment Test), College Scholarship Search Profile, and AP tests are products of the College Board.

College Scholarship Search Profile (CSS Profile). A financial aid form used by many private colleges to award private, non-federal funds.

Common Application. The Common Application is an undergraduate college admissions application that applicants may use to apply to more than nine hundred member colleges and universities in all fifty states and the District of Columbia and in Canada, China, Japan, and many European countries.

cost of attendance. The total cost of college for one year as a full-time student. This covers the cost of tuition, room and board, books, transportation, and personal expenses.

credit. Credits, also known as "semester hours," are earned when students successfully complete a college class. A full-time college student is usually defined as someone who attends three to four classes a term and earns at least twelve credits per term.

CSS Profile. *See* College Scholarship Search Profile (CSS Profile).

cumulative record. The complete record of all courses and grades earned by a student. A student's transcript is a copy of their cumulative record.

defer. For students who apply Early Decision or Early Action, a school may decide not to admit or deny them at first but may defer making a decision and reevaluate the applicant among the general pool of applicants.

degree. A certificate indicating satisfactory completion of a program of study. A four-year degree is typically a BA (bachelor of arts) or a BS (bachelor of science). A graduate degree beyond a bachelor's may be an MA (master of arts) or an MS (master of science). There are also a law degree (JD, or doctor of jurisprudence), a medical degree (MD, or doctor of medicine), a PhD (doctor of philosophy), and many others.

Early Action. A nonbinding admissions plan whereby students apply in October or November and receive a decision within thirty to ninety days.

Early Decision. A binding admissions plan in which the student, parents, and counselor all agree, in writing, that if the student is admitted, they will attend. Deadlines are typically in November for Early Decision I and January for Early Decision II. With both plans, students receive a decision within approximately six weeks.

expected family contribution (EFC). The amount of money that federal and institutional financial aid formulas determine a family can afford to pay for college.

FAFSA (Free Application for Federal Student Aid). Completing this form allows applicants to apply for financial aid in the form of scholarships, grants, loans, and work-study.

Federal Direct Loan. Formerly known as a Stafford Loan, this is a loan from the US government for student financial aid.

fee waiver. Students who register to take a standardized test or who submit an application to a college can apply to be relieved of having to pay the associated fee. This request is often granted when a family's income falls below a certain threshold.

financial aid. Scholarships, grants, loans, and work-study programs allow students to attend college when their families demonstrate a need for additional money to pay for college. Financial aid packages are determined by a family's financial need as measured by their assets, liabilities, and debt-to-income ratio. Some financial aid is also determined by the availability of government funds.

grade point average (GPA). The total number of grade points earned divided by the number of credits taken.

grant. Financial aid that does not need to be repaid. It is usually awarded based on need or academic achievement or a special skill, talent, or heritage.

International Baccalaureate. A course of study that allows high school students to satisfy the curricular admissions requirements of universities in more than seventy countries.

liberal arts college. A college where the emphasis of the curricula is on philosophy, literature, history, languages, and basic science.

major. A student's primary field of study.

master's degree. The degree given for completing a one- to two-year course of study beyond a bachelor's degree. Some examples: master of arts (MA), master of science (MS), master of business administration (MBA), and master of fine arts (MFA).

minor. A subject-area emphasis earned by completing a certain number of credits in an area outside a student's major.

part-time student. A college student who takes fewer than a full-time schedule of classes (usually twelve to sixteen units, or credit hours, per term); part-time status may make students ineligible for financial aid.

Pell Grant. Financial aid from the federal government available to students with significant financial need at many types of colleges and vocational schools.

prerequisite. Courses, test scores, and/or grade level that must be completed or attained before a student is permitted to enroll in a particular course.

private college. A college that is not supported by state taxes.

provisional acceptance. Acceptance to a college that pends submission of a final GPA, proof of graduation, or some other documentation of a student's scholastic record.

PSAT/NMSQT (Preliminary Scholastic Aptitude Test / National Merit Scholarship Qualifying Test). A shortened version of the SAT offered in October to high school juniors and younger. The scores offer an initial assessment for college planning and may help students qualify for National Merit Scholarships.

REA (Restrictive Early Action) / SCEA (Single-Choice Early Action). Offered by several elite colleges such as Harvard,

Princeton, and Yale, REA allows students to receive an admissions decision early with a nonbinding application. When students apply REA, they cannot also apply Early Decision at other schools.

regular decision. The standard admissions plan with application deadlines usually between January 1 and March 30.

rolling admissions. The ongoing review of applications without a formal deadline. The earlier a student applies, the earlier they will be notified of a decision. Colleges accept as many students as they need to fill an incoming class.

ROTC (Reserve Officers Training Corps). Many colleges have ROTC programs that offer years of military training culminating in an officer's commission. At some colleges, credits for ROTC courses can be applied toward a degree. ROTC scholarships, which pay for full college costs, are available.

SAT (Scholastic Assessment Test). A college admissions exam measuring critical reading and math reasoning skills.

scholarship. A gift of money (which does not need to be repaid) given in recognition of student financial need or achievement, skills, or talent.

school profile. This document, produced by high schools, provides school demographic information, curriculum, GPA and class rank calculation, extracurricular activities offered, and other information about the school to give admissions offices an understanding of what was available to an applicant in high school.

Student Aid Report. A form distributed by the College Scholarship Service for the purpose of estimating the family contribution to a student's college costs.

superscoring. Taking SAT or ACT subscores from different test administrations to assemble the highest combined score.

test-blind. Institutions that do not factor standardized test scores in their admissions decisions even if applicants submit them are said to be test-blind.

test-optional. Institutions that do not require standardized test scores for admissions are said to be test-optional. These institutions will, however, review scores from applicants who opt to submit them.

transcript. An official copy of a student's high school or college courses taken and the grades they earned.

transfer courses. College courses that may be transferred to another college.

tuition. The fee for instruction at a college or vocational school.

waitlist. Colleges admit, reject, or waitlist applicants. Depending on how many admitted students accept the offer to attend, colleges can admit students from the waiting list.

weighted course. An admissions policy applied to high school students' GPAs that rewards difficult classes taken.

work-study. A federally funded program that makes part-time jobs available to students with demonstrated financial need.

Index

COLLEGE GUIDES FROM HOPKINS PRESS

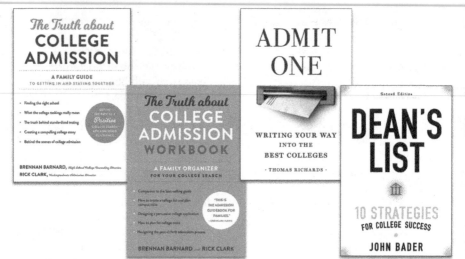

The Truth about College Admission

A Family Guide to Getting In and Staying Together

Brennan Barnard and Rick Clark

"This book provides a comprehensive, practical guide for families, with insights from both the high school and university sides of the experience."—*Forbes*

The Truth about College Admission Workbook

A Family Organizer for Your College Search

Brennan Barnard and Rick Clark

Finally! A workbook that guides you—and your family—through a positive college admission experience.

Admit One

Writing Your Way into the Best Colleges

Thomas Richards

How to craft a dynamic personal essay that will get your college application noticed.

Dean's List

Ten Strategies for College Success, 2nd Ed.

John Bader

You've gotten into college. This is the book you need to succeed.

press.jhu.edu